Slim's
Burma Boys

SLIM'S
BURMA BOYS

by

John Hill

British Library Cataloguing in Publication Data:
A catalogue record for this book is available
from the British Library

Copyright © The estate John Hill 2007

ISBN 978-1-86227-407-5

First published in the UK in 2007 by
Spellmount Limited
Cirencester Road Chalford
Stroud Gloucestershire GL6 8PE

Tel: 01285 730000
Fax: 01285 760001
E-mail: enquiries@spellmount.com
Website: www.spellmount.com

1 3 5 7 9 8 6 4 2

The right of John Hill to be identified
as the author of this work has been asserted by him
in accordance with the Copyright, Designs
and Patents Act 1988

Printed in Great Britain

Contents

Foreword

Slim's Burma Boys relates the personal experiences of men who fought the 'Forgotten War' of the Burma Campaign in the Second World War. Although it supplements John Hill's excellent *China Dragons*, which HRH The Duke of Edinburgh, Prince Philip described in his foreword as 'a worthy addition to the proud history of war', it stands alone as a personal account. Hill wanted his readers to know what it was like to be there. With this in mind, he selected a variety of operations and events from his own B Company, 2nd Battalion Royal Berkshire Regiment.

John Hill, the commander of B Company, was one of only forty-nine who survived out of the original 196 men of B Company who crossed the border into Burma in 1944. The company earned two Military Crosses, a Distinguished Conduct Medal, four Military Medals, and two Mentioned in Dispatches. Writing with first-hand knowledge, Hill conveys what it was like to be a part of the action and experience the adrenalin rush, the fear and courage of those who took part in swollen river crossings, patrols, ambushes, skirmishes, and major actions against a ruthless and determined enemy who would never surrender. His memoir is of general interest, as well as a fitting memorial to his men. It should be prescribed reading for all would-be officers and soldiers. It offers an insight into the need for continuous training and obedience to orders, whatever the circumstances. It explains the dreadful conditions in the jungles and mountains of Burma where disease and climate inevitably took their toll. It records the great fortitude and courage of all those who participated in that war.

Colonel John Hill MC, had not fully prepared *Slim's Burma Boys* for publication before he died at eighty-three years of age. It has been left to family members and regimental friends to complete his work. We are indebted to him for writing this book and to his family for publishing it. Thanks to men like John Hill the 'Forgotten War' will not be forgotten.

Major General D.T. Crabtree CB
Former Colonel
The Duke of Edinburgh's Royal Regiment
(Berkshire and Wiltshire)

Acknowledgements and Editor's Note

Given that John Hill's long and active life ended, sadly enough, shortly before this book was to be submitted to a publisher, it is not surprising that several people have contributed to its belated but welcome appearance. First to be mentioned is his granddaughter Lucy, who with loving care typed a full edition and compiled all parts of the book. Next, John sought the advice of his friend and exemplary military historian, Professor Richard Holmes. We are grateful to him for the detailed and clear advice he gave as to what minor changes in style and context would aid its acceptance by a readership probably born long after those with fading memories of the Second World War. We should also mention our gratitude to his two daughters, Mrs Jackie Cant and Mrs Monica Butt, who have been, from the beginning, most enthusiastic about the necessity of publishing this book in order to honour their father and the soldiers who served under his sure command.

This project was handed over to David Chilton, Curator of the Wardrobe Military Museum, who has successfully published several books by members of their original regiments. Vivian Ridley, one of a number of wardrobe volunteers, took on the task of detailed revision of the text, in line with Richard Holmes' specific suggestions. To make this as straightforward as possible, Mrs Sian Bacon, another volunteer, re-typed the complete text into MS Word format; and a fine job she made of it. Next, the advice was sought of Martin McIntyre, a former Warrant Officer of the Duke of Edinburgh's Royal Regiment, who has a special aptitude for the selection and improvement of dated photographs. Before submission to the publisher, another invaluable task was undertaken by volunteer Miss Naomi Shukman, who carefully scanned all the illustrations and their captions. Lastly, the text was re-checked for errors by Bernard Noble, AFC Squadron Leader (Rtd).

All notes or further explanations of the text have been grouped together at the end of the book in two Appendices. The author obtained permission from the Imperial War Museum to publish some of their photographs, for which we offer our thanks.

Finally, we are very grateful to a former colonel of the regiment and close friend of the author, Major General Derek Crabtree, for writing the foreword to this unique work.

John Hill was born in Christchurch, Hampshire. Educated at Clifton College and Sandhurst, he won two half blues for Pentathalon and Rowing and a prize for tactics. Commmissioned into the Royal Berkshire Regiment in 1938, he was posted to the Second Battalion in India. He saw active service in Burma and won the Military Cross. After the war his service included postings to the School of Infantry, Egypt, Germany and to Cyprus for the EOKA Emergency, where he received a Mention in Dispatches.

Preface

The title *Slim's Burma Boys* came from a chance remark made on the occasion of the VJ Parade in 1995 for the fiftieth anniversary of the final end of the Second World War. Arriving in London to join the 14th Army Contingent of veterans on Horseguard's Parade, I asked a senior police officer if he knew where the 14th Army Contingent would assemble. He said, '14th Army. Oh don't you mean "Slim's Burma Boys"?' Field Marshal Sir William Slim, or 'Bill' to all who served in the 14th Army which he had commanded so brilliantly, would have been delighted that an onlooker should refer in this way to the men he had commanded. Down-to-earth informality set the scene for most of those who served under him. So here is an opportunity for some of 'Slim's Burma Boys' to tell their own stories.

Ten of the following chapters provide close insight into active service conditions and of fiercely contested actions of an infantry rifle company in Burma during the Second World War. Neither over-glamorised or understated, the themes of these stories are as relevant today as they were more than sixty years ago. Typical of these are service to others, courage in adversity, dedication to duty, physical and mental endurance, all of which are bound together by cheerful self-sacrifice and self-discipline. These are bedrock principles for all human enterprise and endeavour, worth retelling as the twentieth century has drawn to a close. Although the world is now free from the risk of conflicts between world powers, it is now, however, deeply disturbed by international terrorism. Still a world in which service-inspired qualities are sometimes forgotten by young and old alike, these qualities

1. The author, John Hill, during the war.

may be called upon again today. It is a matter of great pride that so many of our countrymen, from all walks of life, worked together, often under conditions of great hardship and danger, to help in the defeat of an efficient and ruthless military machine, the Japanese Imperial Army.

The eleventh chapter of this book draws together some important aspects of soldiering whose themes ran through all our activities. As these are seldom discussed in any depth, this chapter gives them an airing. The final chapter describes a memorable return visit to Burma and the celebrations in the UK on the fiftieth anniversary of the end of the war with Japan.

John Hill

List of Maps and Illustrations

Introduction

After the end of the Battle of France, the retreat from Dunkirk and the ensuing total war in Europe, it was inevitable that the defence of the UK would become the overwhelming priority of the British government. Thereafter, the slow but steady recovery of lost land and the defeat of the German Armies in North Africa, Sicily and Italy kept pressure on the Axis Powers, while long-term preparations for the eventual invasion of the European continent were made. Even after Japan's attack on Pearl Harbor and her successful invasions of several countries of South-East Asia, fighting the Japanese in Asia was to remain a low priority compared to the war in Europe. In practical terms, those serving in Burma felt themselves to be 'The Forgotten Army'. Despite the arduous conditions which prevailed, and the perceived tenacity and cruelty of the Japanese, operations were more distant, less spectacular. The operations were certainly less significant if measured by the delivery of up-to-date weaponry, such as armoured vehicles and the latest aircraft, as well as the lack of attention of the media.

In spite of these somewhat negative observations, by May 1945, when the European War had ended, some 750,000 men and women from Britain and the Commonwealth and Empire were immersed in the struggle for military supremacy against the Japanese in the India/Burma theatre of operations. A hazard of the environment, apart from the dense undergrowth encountered in the jungles, was the ubiquitous bamboo. Growing in large clumps, often twenty feet or more in height, the thick stems and bunched leaves created impassable terrain in many areas. Movement could only be made by cutting through the stems, thus slowing progress. Each man carried a dah, a long, broad knife, which was frequently used both in the advance and when preparing defensive positions. In soldiering terms, the terrain thus involved almost every category of military operations, namely mountain warfare, plains and village fighting, river-crossing and of course endless jungle warfare. Commando-style raids over fast-flowing rivers and severe problems in reinforcement and resupply were characteristic of all areas. Truly it can be said that soldiers in the Burma Campaign needed as wide a range of skills as in any other theatre of war.

The Allied Armies in India and Burma represented a unique brotherhood in the nations of the British, Indian, Gurkhas, East and West Africans, Malayans, Burmese and others, embracing many races and religious faiths. The United States supplied vital air and administrative backup in the later stages when elements of the Chinese Army also joined the Allied effort.

These events took place at a time when comradely support for each other and unselfish behaviour by the great majority of combatants were commonplace. In the Far East, the bonds of humanity, kinship and of co-operation in the face of brutality, loss of life and of friends gave those who remained the moral and spiritual uplift needed at the sharp end of battle. Against a background of chronic tropical diseases, enervating climatic conditions and the paucity of medical stores, a steely will to survive in all circumstances was engendered. Far away from homes and families, high morale was a prerequisite.

Throughout the land battles in the 14th Army area of north-west and central Burma, as well as the 15 Corps area of the Arakan, soldiers in forward units, whether African, Indian, Gurkha or British, mostly marched and fought carrying all their needs and emergency supplies on their backs. A few Jeeps and trailers, mule trains of varying sizes and a valuable air supply organisation gave the vital administrative backup to maintain the advance over the hundreds of miles covered. In the intense heat, through the jungles, across the great rivers over the vast hills and mountains, and astride the seldom-used dirt tracks and under-developed roads, B Company, 2nd Battalion Royal Berkshire Regiment, was just one element among the battalions, brigades and divisions which waged this total war. As part of the 14th Army in the 19th Indian (Dagger) Division, similar activities to those related here occurred in many units, but this account under the title *Slim's Burma Boys* dedicates itself to the real-life experiences of the officers, NCOs and men of B Company in eight isolated situations, offered as examples of soldiering 'over there'. Typically, these randomly selected examples demonstrate the day-to-day activities in contact with the enemy, as well as large-scale, set-piece operations.

These isolated situations do not therefore refer to the major engagements where carefully planned attacks, supported by British and Indian gunners, Sikh machine-gunners and our own battalion mortars, involved the whole battalion. In these engagements, B Company was heavily committed, marking the high points of a series of tough, volatile and fast-moving actions. All of these, without exception, exposed each man to direct small-arms and shell fire, while attacks across bullet-swept scrub and open ground were made. Higher levels of casualties inevitably resulted compared to those incurred from 'routine' patrols and when returning fire from dug-in positions.

In just three of our major battles, the casualties in B Company were as follows:

Location	KIA	Wounded	Totals
KIN-U (48 hrs)	6	11	17
KABWET (10 days)	7	18	25
MANDALAY (14 days)	10	21	31
Totals	23	50	73

Full details of the total numbers killed, missing or died of wounds, or who were wounded throughout the campaign, together with the names of those killed, are shown in Appendix 2, Annex E.

It must be said at the outset that the infantry, as in most operations, were supported by a large number of other arms and services, all co-ordinated by higher HQ staff officers. Without such support, these campaigns would be impossible. Inevitably, in Burma soldiers from other arms and services become immersed, from time to time, in frontline infantry fighting. All infantrymen, everywhere in this theatre of operations, acknowledged this vital support and involvement in enabling objectives to be gained and ascendancy over the Japanese to be won, both in attack and defence.

Behind, but often up with B Company's deployments, came the gunners of 115 Field Regiment, RA with their 25lb guns, controlled and fired by dedicated teams of forward observation officers, who lived with us for much of the time. Likewise, there were groups from the 33rd Anti-Tank Regiment, RA with their 3in mortars. Periodically, crews in their light tanks from the 7th and later 8th Indian Cavalry, as well as Sikh machine-gunners from the 11th Sikh Regiment, joined us.

Engineers from the 20th Bombay Sappers and Miners, Indian Army, carried out bridge-building, road-making and mine-clearance operations. Interspersed down the line, Royal Signals, Royal Army Service Corps, Royal Electrical and Mechanical Engineers, as well as Royal Army Medical Corps units, all co-ordinated by commanders and their staff officers, were often well to the fore and involved in day-to-day operations.

To all these supporting units, fell the task of keeping up the speed of advance and maintaining support in whatever we did or wherever we went. Co-ordinated battle plans were made to gain maximum advantage over the Japanese, invariably integrating the forward elements of all these groups, who, from time to time, became as heavily involved as we were. Typical of these were Air Observation Posts on foot, controlling fire support from Auster light aircraft, both for field guns and B25 bombers, as well as for Spitfires and Hurribombers, which also became vulnerable from enemy anti-aircraft fire at the sharp end of our ground battle.

While the enemy's grenades, rifles and machine-guns were largely directed at the infantry, the shells from his guns were no respecter of persons, falling on soldiers at the front and rear indiscriminately, irrespective of their operations or administrative duties. Despite these factors, it is interesting to find that the casualty lists of the 19th Indian Division show that over 80 per cent of all men killed or wounded were from the infantry. B Company received its share of casualties. Between November 1944 and June 1945, from a total of 196 men, all ranks of the original men who crossed the Chindwin river into Burma, or who were posted as reinforcements, thirty-nine were killed or died of wounds or missing, and seventy-three were wounded. Some thirty-five were evacuated due to sickness or other reasons. Fifty of all ranks thus survived to tell all or part of the tale. The need for officers and NCOs to command from the front was paramount in the jungle and close country, and so a disproportionate number became casualties. In B Company, the killed included an officer, a company sergeant major, a company quartermaster sergeant and six sergeants. Our wounded included four officers and six sergeants. Command in battle, in Burma, took a heavy toll of our leaders.

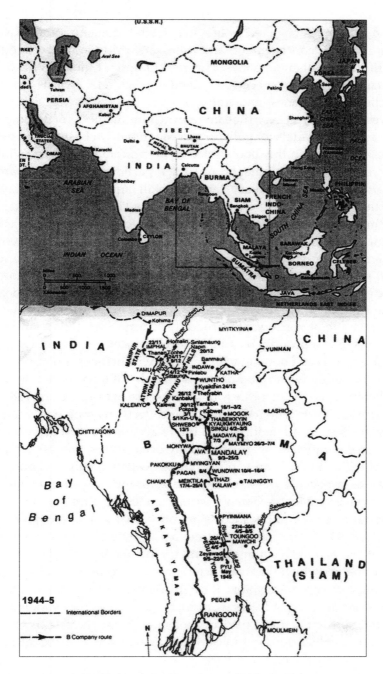

2. *Two maps showing the position of Burma in South-East Asia. Topographical details and other information are described in the introduction.*

In most armies engaged in life-and-death battle situations, participants obtain encouragement, and units take pride in the recognition
of skilful and gallant activities. This recognition for those on the firing
line usually results in special commendations. Medal awards testify of
a soldier's effectiveness and courage.

As can also be seen from the same annex, nine members of B Company
were awarded medals for gallantry, or Mentioned in Dispatches. In the
events described in this book, selected at random from many similar
skirmishes and engagements, no other participants were awarded
medals for their exemplary tenacity, skill and behaviour. Having
read the stories, you may well ask, 'Why not?' One needs to realise
that 'medals' in this context means awards for gallantry, such as the
Distinguished Conduct Medal or the Military Medal, as distinct from
the campaign medals awarded solely for service in a theatre of operations. The Burma Star War Medal was essentially given as recognition
of the presence of a soldier in the theatre at any time during the period
of the campaign, regardless of his activity or unit. All those present
in this theatre of war were awarded the Burma Star. Today, survivors
wear this medal proudly on suitable occasions.

Rich rewards and notable achievements within the sections, platoons
and companies which composed a British infantry battalion were
amply rewarded by the professionalism, sense of purpose and camara-
derie among those who individually or collectively took part. Support
for each other in the field, where many acts of bravery, self sacrifice
and true comradeship were often daily occurrences, was an accepted
part of regimental life and spirit. Where deeds were judged and confirmed as especially outstanding and appropriate gallantry medals
were awarded. Most recipients would agree that these medals were
recognition of their unit's success, in individual actions as much as of
their own. However, many 'routine' battle activities involving brave
and selfless actions went unsung and undocumented in this fast-moving campaign, which was conducted on wide fronts and at the end of
long lines of communication. Recognised by the award of gallantry
medals or not, many soldiers working alone or together by their initiative and spirited actions, gave of their best in the interest of all. The
true stories which follow indicate the degree to which the so-called
'ordinary men' played their part.

There is no doubt that similar events to those described here were
repeated in many infantry units in this theatre of operations, but this
account is centred on the men in B Company, 2nd Battalion Royal

Berkshire Regiment alone. In these accounts, the perspectives and events themselves are all based on actual combat encounters, in a hostile tropical environment and against a cruel enemy.

In my book, *China Dragons*, published by Cassell in 1991, I described the activities of the 2nd Battalion Royal Berkshire Regiment in India and Burma, and the long training which preceded our entry into Burma with the 19th Indian Division. That book covered our major actions, tactics and movements through the country, touching only lightly on the life of the individual soldier. It did not illustrate in detail the many occasions when our men were embroiled in life-threatening situations. *Slim's Burma Boys* is intended to fill this important gap by giving descriptions of some examples of real-life events in this soldier's war, and of the thoughts and aspirations of those who were involved.

By 1944 the skill, ruthlessness and military superiority of the Japanese soldier was well documented and understood. The previous three years of retreats and defeats of the Allies had posed questions as to the ability of the British Army to overcome this enemy. New lessons had to be learnt the hard way. Long and closely focused training had led to a huge turnaround in the ability and confidence of Allied soldiers. By the end of 1944, no one doubted the effort required or sacrifices needed to turn the tables on the Japanese. In November 1944, as B Company went into action, spirits and confidence were high.

CHAPTER 1

A River Crossing –
Rescue of the Signaller

The last training-for-war-exercise was in its final stage. The commander of B Company finished his briefing by saying, 'Make sure you get the lamp across intact and keep the batteries dry.' Corporal Howlett, commanding the patrol of just four men, which was to include Dickens the signaller, smiled wryly to himself. The monsoon had been on for a week. The streams had swollen to rivers and rivers into torrents. The warm rain at that moment was beating down on the canvas of the makeshift cover above their heads, while water seeped in under the edges, flowing in over the 2ft-deep trench which had been dug round the bamboo framework as a 'monsoon drain'.

The moist map in his hands showed that the river he was to cross was some thirty yards wide and seven feet six inches deep at the point selected for the crossing, with a current of 3 to 5 knots. Two intelligence reports just received briefly stated, 'all rivers rising, roads marked "liable to flooding in monsoon" now effective'. He glanced at his map. The last two roads within one mile of the river were annotated neatly, 'liable to flooding in monsoon'. There were to be no boats. 'If you have to swim, carry out the usual drill; wrap your kit in your ground sheets and take extra sheets for the lamp and batteries,' the company commander said. Keep the batteries dry indeed! Howlett remembered their training in India two years before, and these events were vivid in his memory. In both years, the monsoon broke on them, finding the whole battalion deep in tropical jungle country, very similar to their present area. Being unable to keep dry for three weeks on the first occasion and for ten days on the second, most of the men became unfit to march due to foot rot or 'fiery feet', as the men called it, because of its effect of turning the skin pink and raw. They lived in conditions only fit for ducks, as they seemed to spend most of their time fully immersed. They had come through training with a vast amount of experience of how to exist under conditions of almost continuous submersion from the heavens. At the same time, they managed to wrestle and force their way with mules, Jeeps and full equipment over, through and often under the raging torrents which cascaded and slashed at the narrow gullies, which created dangerous hazards in crossings. Now here they were again in the 1944 Indian monsoon, completing their last training before moving to join the 14th Army to face the Japanese in Burma.

Howlett, twenty-three, from London's East End, was strong, fit and cheerful. After three years in India he had adapted to everything the Army had thrown at him. Now here he was at the last training area about to take four men out on patrol on a hill about six miles away to send back information on 'enemy' movement on an ominous-looking, craggy outcrop of rock.

The lamp and its battery were the key to success of this mission. Being wireless, signals in Morse from this lamp would be the only means of sending back information to the company commander. 'Keep the batteries dry!' They had often done the impossible before, so why not again? 'OK', he thought, he would give it his best shot.

He found Dickens, Thompson, Bailey and Reynolds sheltering under their groundsheets which had long since ceased to shelter them, except to keep their wet clothes and bodies warm. Wrapping the heavy Aldis lamp with its 12-volt battery in the extra groundsheets, they strapped them into two large packs and lashed them to a stout bamboo pole. Dickens and Thompson carried the pole, while Bailey moved a few yards ahead as lead scout. Howlett, with map and compass, stationed himself in the centre as Reynolds acted as rear protection, following a few paces to the rear. Setting off down an ill-defined muddy track, they soon squelched and sloshed their way out of sight into the heavy jungle. The going was better than he had dared to hope. Twice in the two miles to the river they had to wade up to their armpits through muddy streams with the water tugging at their feet, holding their weapons and equipment above their heads. Dickens, the smallest of them, had nearly fallen but kept on his feet by clutching at Thompson and the pole. Dickens, a silent man, spent much of his time apparently thinking about home, though no one was quite sure. However, one thing all were certain about was that he was a first-class signaller; a man to be respected. Before the war, he had had a good job with a famous radio manufacturing company.

The sound of tons of water moving fast in a confined space, accentuated by the tall trees reaching sixty to eighty feet above their heads, was like thunder as they pushed through the last of the dank undergrowth to come close to the river bank. Howlett, satisfied that the enemy was not openly visible in this simulated exercise, weighed up the situation. It was not very encouraging, even for those used to such conditions. Crawling back to the patrol he carefully outlined his plan for the crossing. He went through the routine – describing the enemy situation, the importance of getting over, their task on the other side of the river, the method of crossing, the place they would strip and prepare for the swim and the action they would all take if they were surprised. The river thundered and roared as the rain steadily poured. Howlett couldn't help but ominously think that the elements were warning him not to try them too far. Finishing the orders with the usual, 'Any questions?', Thompson, Bailey and Reynolds nodded 'OK'. Quietly, and with his eyes showing no emotion, Dickens announced, 'I can't swim, Corp!'

They had no alternative but to swim and struggle to cross the river out of their depth against that current. Howlett knew better than any of them that they could be scattered, buffeted and half drowned. He knew they would land possibly 400 to 600 yards down stream on the other bank, if, in fact, they got over this mad, raging deluge. They had crossed many such rivers in their long training. Six men had lost their lives, due to accidents, but now they were alone. There were no safety boats or ropes. They could not wait until the river subsided, as they had done on some of their other training exercises. This was the final realistic exercise before meeting the Japanese. Realism was now essential.

'It's about time you woke up and told us you couldn't swim, mate,' Howlett addressed Dickens in a few, short kind words. 'We'll make it, Corp.' Thompson, a large, fair-haired man of twenty-five and a strong swimmer said, 'I'll give Dickens a hand.' Howlett replied, 'He'll need more than a hand. He'll need bloody water wings.'

As they moved to their take-off point, Howlett decided they could only succeed in the crossing if they kept together, around some central flotation. The jungle was scattered with bamboo growths. On arrival at their rendezvous, they lashed two more 6ft-long lengths of bamboo to the lamp and battery. Stripping themselves down to their pants and carefully wrapping their boots, clothes, Sten guns, equipment

3. *Crossing a chaung (stream) on a makeshift bridge constructed of local materials showing an unusually placid stream in the dry season.*

and ammunition in separate ground sheet bundles, they tied all the bundles together to the poles with ropes that each man always carried. They moved slowly into the water. To add buoyancy, all water bottles were emptied and tied around the bundles.

The raging river had swollen to almost twice its width as shown on the map, now sixty yards across. Turgid, swirling water with small tree trunks and debris tumbling about added to the hazard. The water was not cold, but Howlett noticed Dickens shivering as they pushed their bundles of gear into the torrent. It was apparent that they would be swept off their feet after about twenty yards when they reached the normal river bed. Stumbling and cursing, they moved on. The bundle floated well, and even when Howlett put his full weight on it, the bundle remained buoyant, with the water bottles bobbing like corks. While giving orders for the crossing, Howlett told Dickens to grip the bamboo poles and not to let go. Thompson and Reynolds were to pull from the front, while he and Bailey, who was a weaker swimmer, pushed from behind. At all costs, Dickens and the lamp, with its battery, had to reach the far bank. He could see that Dickens did not need to be retold, for he was already clamped like a leech to the bundle.

After ten or fifteen yards, they were still surprisingly on their feet, the water around their waists swirling and tugging, fighting them every inch of the way. A small tree trunk hit them. Thompson suddenly sank up to his shoulders, and with him went Reynolds. In no time, they were all swept off their feet and twisting and leaping, the bundle with Dickens and Bailey on top and the other three mostly under it, were moving fast into the main stream. Striking out for the far bank took all of their energy and it seemed to Howlett that they had little hope of making much progress across, although their speed downstream was spectacular. Dickens, resigned and unable to take an active part, held on tightly and kept his head. Bailey fell off once, tried to get back, fell off again, but somehow regained his hold and even managed to kick a few strokes. The far bank seemed no nearer. They were moving even faster downstream, but the makeshift raft was serving them well, even if it bucked and pitched like a mad mule. The heavy battery gave some stability, acting like a bulky keel. Crisis then happened. The rope lashing the bundles to the poles parted, becoming three separate bundles. The strain had been too much, even for their strongest knots. With some fifteen yards still to go, Howlett shouted to Dickens, 'Hold on,' and then

4. Crossing a chaung the hard way. Manhandling a Jeep over one of many rivers.

to the others he shouted, 'Make for the bank.' Thompson and he then attached themselves to the main bundle containing the lamp, the battery and Dickens. Bailey shouted that he was going down but hung on to one of the bundles, and Reynolds remained attached to another. Both soon disappeared downstream in a flurry of foam, legs and arms.

The dead weight of Dickens and the lamp kept the central precious bundle low in the water, dangerously low, Howlett thought as they fought on. Water cascaded over him as he took in several mouthfuls and was blinded by spray, but they lunged on. He was tired but had no option but to keep going. Suddenly, one of the poles struck an underwater obstacle, reared up in the air and, with a shout, Dickens let go his hold. In no time, Dickens was swept away from the bundle. The worst had happened. Howlett acted quickly. With a few strong strokes, Howlett was alongside Dickens, but Dickens, now badly frightened, seized him and tried to clutch his head. Thus locked together and drinking water, they sank from sight. Thompson, still with his bundle, could see their grim struggle – first, Howlett's head, then Dickens', then a leg or arm, then spray and foam, then nothing. The water raged on. Thompson, pushing the bundle, felt the pulling, tearing torrent slackening. He could no longer see the others. Kicking and pulling with his arms, the water still pouring over and round him, he suddenly found his feet touching ground. He was over. His relief was unbounded, for he had nearly decided he would have to turn back. But where were the others? With the water receding from him, Thompson slowly rose higher until he was waist deep. There he could see some 100 yards below two figures close together in the water, also moving slowly towards the bank. As he looked, he realised they were Howlett and Dickens, for they had no supporting bundle. 'Thought they'd had it,' he said to himself. 'The Corp made it.' Then he looked at the bundle with the lamp and battery still bobbing and dancing in the water in front of him, as he tugged and shoved it towards the land. 'Not much bleeding good without Dicky,' he said almost aloud to the bundle. Moving more freely now, he at last pulled his load above the water line. Exhausted as he was, without boots and naked, but for his pants, he stumbled down the bank towards the other two. As he got nearer, he saw they were both all in. Dickens was leaning against Howlett, who was hardly moving. Plunging in, Thompson reached them. 'Hold him up,' Howlett managed to murmur. 'Get him out of the water.' Grabbing Dickens, Thompson pulled and half-carried him further away from the clutching, sucking water, into the shallows.

Howlett, recovering as he moved, spluttered, 'Thought we were a gonner. Dicky tried to drown me, but we made it.' Shuddering and gasping for air, his face almost grey, Howlett no longer looked the fit man he had been before the crossing. They stumbled on through the shallows, dragging Dickens, who was conscious but waterlogged, to collapse on the first piece of ground they could see. 'Pump Dicky out,' Howlett said. Turning him over on his front brought up most of the water he had swallowed.

Thompson worked on Dickens rhythmically, pressing his body down into the mud and keeping his head clear of obstruction. Soon, Dickens showed signs of life. They sat him up and he too emptied himself of some of the contents of the river. Shortly, rubbing Dickens' hands and body and moving his limbs, they were able to get him on his feet and together they moved off to regain the bundle left by Thompson.

For three to four minutes, Corporal Howlett and Dickens fought the battle of their lives against the relentless, rushing river, and won. Dickens said, 'Thanks, Corp, sorry I couldn't make it.' Howlett replied, with no humour in his voice, 'You'll learn to swim when we get out of this. A good thing there were no Japs this time.' As they collected themselves, looking downstream, two dishevelled figures could be seen staggering through the shallows, dragging themselves and their bundles. Although totally exhausted, Bailey and Reynolds were safe. The team was complete again. Messages could now get through. When they collected themselves, they could complete their mission. The river, cheated of its prey, poured angrily past them. The rain streamed down from above as they opened up the bundle and recovered their soggy clothes and equipment.

This final rehearsal before they crossed the Chindwin river into Burma had brought out the best in Corporal Howlett and his small group of soldiers. Here was great dedication and selflessness by brave men under extreme pressure. Involuntarily perhaps, but none the less certainly, past training and understanding of the possible hazards that would have to be met, countered and overcome, had proved their worth. These were horrendous experiences by any normal standards, but the message remained clear as these men of B Company finished their apprenticeship, their duty done before joining the 14th Army, becoming 'Slim's Burma Boys'.

CHAPTER 2

Recovery of a Casualty under Fire

Most people might believe that the training of soldiers for war has nothing in common with the square bashing, barrack room inspections, ceremonial parades, the saluting of officers and other apparent infringements of human freedom and sensitivity. Such people are perhaps unaware of the psychological and personal qualities involved in the struggle for supremacy over an enemy in the field, against the instinct of self preservation in a real battle. In war, how best can one expect a normal, average sensible young man to face the most extreme personal danger, willingly? When in such dire circumstances, how can one think only how best to help other men defeat the immediate enemy, without a thought of saving his own neck?

Much is owed to those who succeed in overcoming their fears and instinctively carry out their duty, striving under conditions impossible to comprehend under normal circumstances. Analyse as you will, in the last resort, when weary limbs and minds are in charge, it is the solid grounding of discipline, based on attention to detail and obedience of orders, that carries the faltering through. In the British Army, such a state of mind owes much to regimental *esprit de corps* and to routine disciplines on the parade ground as well as in the barrack room.

This is a story of self sacrifice and bravery of high order, displayed by two wartime soldiers of B Company, when, without the qualities induced by these traditional methods, another man would have fallen into the hands of the Japanese.

It was Boxing Day 1944. Some sixty miles north of Mandalay, the leading infantry platoons were moving south towards the city against

31

stiffening Japanese resistance. In B Company, some men had marched nearly 300 miles from the Indian border through the jungle, over two mountain ranges and the 400-yard wide Chindwin river, among other lesser water obstacles. Each soldier carried some 60lb of equipment and belongings on his back. Only during actual attacks were these large packs temporarily discarded, to be collected again after the operation was over. Over Christmas these men were in action and in close contact with the enemy. Shelling, mortar and small arms fire had caused casualties on both sides and during Christmas night, a long encircling move involving the whole company had resulted in the successful ambush of a withdrawing Japanese rearguard.

After three days and nights in close contact with the enemy, elated but both wary and tired, 6 Platoon was once again on the move, leading the column astride the narrow track, which served as their centre line through the open jungle and small clearings in their path. Privates Stokes and Caswell moved skilfully ahead on either side of the track, weapons at the ready, trained eyes watching for the slightest sign of the Japanese. Making steady progress, they arrived at a small clearing. There, not more than fifty yards away, was a Japanese soldier, clearly visible yet unsuspecting. Stokes threw himself to the ground, and before the enemy had time to find cover, he fired a shot, hitting the man instantly.

From across the clearing, almost immediately, close and accurate cross-fire was opened from two light machine-guns and a number of rifles. All their training had taught each man to locate the exact place from which weapons were fired, by the 'thump' which followed the sharp 'crack' as a bullet streaked overhead. The need to listen for the thump was essential to pinpoint the source of the firing. Experience taught them to ignore the crack and listen for that all-important thump. Locating the enemy's firing position, the leading section commander, Corporal 'Chalky' White, decided to seize the initiative and quickly ordered covering fire. He then took Privates Pridham, Smedley, Morgan and Dale, moving fast and wide to the right flank across the clearing, firing their rifles and submachine-guns from the hip. All went well until they were halfway over the open space when, despite the covering fire, they were accurately engaged by the enemy and pinned down in the clearing. Private Smedley was hit in the arm. Realising that the position was too strong and the chance for surprise had gone, Corporal White shouted for more covering fire and then, with his four men, started to withdraw again to their side of the clearing.

Moving back fast, and despite accurate support fire, they were continuously engaged by enemy machine-guns and rifles. A shout told Corporal White that Pridham, who had got closest to the enemy, had been hit. Arriving at the near side of the clearing, while he applied a dressing to Smedley's arm, Corporal White could see the wounded Pridham had dragged himself under a small earth bank about 18in high. Although the enemy was firing shot after shot towards him, he was safe while he stayed there, about ten yards from the nearest Japanese. By this time, as company commander, I had come up quickly and decided that the enemy was too well entrenched in their foxholes and too numerous for the leading 6 Platoon to assault on their own. A company flanking attack, supported by mortars and artillery fire, was the immediate action required. Before the plan of attack could be decided, we had to extricate the wounded Pridham, who had been badly hit and could hardly move without assistance. Meanwhile, close and accurate fire engaged both sides across the clearing.

The method to be used to cross twenty-five yards of bullet-spattered ground in full view, within ten yards of an alert and active enemy, and the lifting of helpless Pridham to a stretcher and recovering him, demanded careful but urgent planning. Speed was essential, for it was now about 2 p.m., and if an attack was to be launched on the enemy before dark, around 6 p.m., then there was little time in which to attempt the rescue of Pridham. Meanwhile, the battalion commanding officer was keen to push on. Should he be left? By now he may have died. Should more lives be at risk to retrieve him? Further bouts of enemy fire kept us all flat on the ground. Some sixty yards back from the clearing, orders were given to rescue Pridham, who was seen to move. So now we could be certain that he was still alive.

Twenty-four smoke grenades, each of which would last approximately twenty seconds, were sent up to Corporal White. Two more Bren* guns were brought into position about fifty yards from the clearing. Six more riflemen were moved up to Corporal White, to overlook the centre of the clearing where Pridham lay. To the right of the clearing, two stretcher bearers were positioned, under cover and ready to go.

The simple plan was for continuous covering fire to be given by the Bren guns, riflemen and grenade dischargers to pin down the enemy in their open foxholes so that they would not be able to use their weapons.

---

* Bren Guns – light machine-guns.

5. Some of B Company before crossing the Chindwin river, November 1944. Among those shown are Lieutenant Ridley; Sergeants Heywood and Barrett; Corporal Stow; Lance Corporals Horton, Brown, Heath and Sion; Privates Murray, Bigginton, Baker, Bunn, Elwell, Dodd, Moore, Lacey, Fuller, Thompson, Stewart, Armsby, Rainsford, Allwright, Leggett and Birch.

Then they were to smother the clearing with smoke grenades and at a signal, for the two stretcher bearers, Privates Pettit and Semple, to move at top speed across the open ground, place Pridham on the stretcher and get back to cover as quickly as possible.

Both stretcher bearers had ample time to realise that they were about to risk their lives for their comrade and that their chances of success were at best fifty-fifty, for they would be within ten yards of a manned Japanese prepared position. Those giving covering fire also knew what was at stake. No one knew the men's feelings better than the company commander. All, instinctively, wanted to save Pridham if it was humanly possible; even the stretcher bearers, who were in the greatest danger, would not accept the impossible. A pause in the battalion's forward movement had to be accepted, despite the frustration of those in the rear.

On a signal, the Bren guns and rifles opened rapid fire across the clearing. At short intervals, the sharp report of the ballistic cartridges, firing high explosive grenades high into the air, began to descend with a crump on the Japanese position. The first of the smoke grenades burst across the clearing, sending thick white clouds of dense, acrid-smelling smoke into the air. It effectively blotted out the far side of the clearing. Although the enemy now opened spasmodic, concentrated fire, it was inaccurate. Up leapt Pettit and Semple, running with the stretcher between them, gaining five, ten, fifteen yards. Suddenly, Pettit fell, tripped by the rough ground. He scrambled to his feet, and in the smoke haze and through the firing, which had reached intense volume from both sides, both men could be seen through the smoke, lifting Pridham and placing him on the stretcher. Next, they lifted the heavy stretcher and turned at an unsteady broken gait, starting the homeward journey. Seconds seemed to become minutes, while those who watched with their hearts thumping saw first Pettit, and then Semple, stumble and fall. Pridham was thrown to the ground with each stumble and made no move as bullets ricocheted, whirring off trees and the ground. Both men laboriously placed him back on the stretcher to continue their journey. Miraculously untouched by enemy fire, gasping and sweating, they were through our forward troops and willing hands took over the carrying of the stretcher with its precious load. Neither Pettit nor Semple would relinquish their charge until they had dressed and bandaged his severe wounds and seen him on his way to the regimental Aid Post to the rear.

Both men then rejoined the Company HQ, as the main attack now began. One man had been saved from certain death by the unflinching bravery of two of his comrades. Two more men had done their duty in the interest of others, steeled and schooled by the routines of the parade ground and barrack rooms.

CHAPTER 3

'Ambush'

In the jungle, one of the most effective ways of inflicting casualties on the enemy is to set up an ambush. The fear of being ambushed by concealed enemy forces inhibits speed of movement and lowers morale. This mode of jungle fighting was frequently put to the test by both sides, with varying degrees of success. Successful ambushes owed much to the training and ability of platoon or section leaders to assess the situation, find suitable sites and cause casualties without cost to their own men. A prerequisite was that reliable information of the enemy's location and movements should be known.

An illustration of two widely different ambushes shows what can and did happen during the advance through central Burma. The first is an example of one of many such incidents, deep in the jungle. The second is about an ambush in the streets of Burma's old capital city, Mandalay.

The city's closely packed, bomb-damaged houses, the intervening scrub, debris and dried-out water courses created a terrain very similar in tactical significance to the jungle. In both cases, visibility was much reduced and fields-of-fire for weapons were severely restricted.

These two examples illustrate the effect of an ambush from different aspects, one unsuccessful, the other a success. Both examples are typical of many similar occasions experienced by the men of B Company across the terrain of central Burma.

6. and 7. Above and opposite: *Typical jungle ambush country.*

An Unsuccessful Ambush in the Jungle

On 3 and 4 January 1945, some three weeks after crossing the Chindwin river at the start of the campaign, B Company was advancing southward near a small village called Kanbalu, astride the main road. The company moved by a wide encircling route through the jungle and light scrub to avoid Japanese rearguards, which were usually sited at the forward edge of a village astride the track. In sparse jungle, some 600 yards to the south of the village, the two leading men, Privates Blowers and Briggs, having seen some clothes hanging on a tree, dropped to the ground and crawled forward. An even more surprising scene confronted them. A recently occupied Japanese position lay before them with lightly dug trenches surrounding several piles of equipment both on the ground and in the trees. There was no sign of anyone, but in the centre evidence of cooking packs, shovels, ammunition, food and water containers with medical stores were scattered around. As the forward section watched, a Japanese soldier was spotted at the far side, partly clothed with his shirt tails flapping, running away towards the village. This set off a string of ribald remarks about the reason for his quick escape with his trousers down!

When the leading section and platoon commanders arrived, it was decided that some dozen enemy had occupied the position and were now probably searching for food in Kanbalu. They would be likely to return to the area before dark. As company commander, I decided that the remainder of the company should halt and form a firm base some 800 yards to the east, while dispositions were to be made to lay an ambush on the approach route. Booby traps were set and a killing area covered by fire from all weapons established astride the enemy position. As darkness fell without sighting or hearing any Japanese, Lance Corporal Brown and some ten men waited patiently in fire positions, sentries having been posted.

At about midnight the ambush party heard movement and, astonishingly, a single Japanese soldier carrying his rifle walked down the track springing the booby trap. Almost immediately behind him, accompanied by short crisp orders and with their rifles firing, some twenty Japanese rushed into the trap from the north-west. This unexpected direction, avoiding the planned ambush, caused chaos. Privates Veale and Briggs opened fire killing the lead enemy. Soon, firing broke out indiscriminately with both sides being interlocked in the dark. Shouts and screams indicated casualties to the enemy, but the ambush as a surprise had failed. Lance Corporal Brown ordered the withdrawal. He already had two men killed and Privates Blowers, Dew and Beale had been wounded. In the dark, shots, shouting and screams continued as all hauled themselves over the 800 yards, helping each other to their base, shouting out the password as they came near. Private Beale, with one leg almost severed, came in later having dragged himself and his machine-gun painfully along the ground for the full distance. There was no follow-up by the enemy, who also seemed to have had enough. One of the reasons for the failure was the jamming of the light machine-gun. Its striker had failed; something which occurred from time to time, despite careful maintenance. During the remainder of the night, explosions were heard from the ambush area, as the bad news was digested and casualties treated.

At first light, the company advanced to the site of the ambush. As some compensation for the loss of two brave soldiers and the wounding of three more, two dead enemy were found beside the pile of packs, three more at the northern entrance to the ambush area and two additional bodies at the southern exit, with the sight of blood on the track indicating further casualties. Privates Blowers, Dew, Beale and Briggs, and others, acted with great presence of mind under Lance

Corporal Brown's leadership. No praise could be too high for Private Beale's heroic action, while severely wounded, in refusing to abandon his light machine-gun. All these gallant men lived to fight another day.

A Successful Ambush in the City of Mandalay

It is 11 March 1945, some ten weeks and 150 miles further after the jungle incident, en route to battles on the Irrawaddy river and the assault on Mandalay City.

We had experienced ten weeks of seemingly endless encounters with the enemy. We had been involved in a major battle, testing us to the limit, at the steamer station of Kabwet, after which, we had a welcome visit from General Bill Slim.

During this visit, a patrol had given a first-hand account of atrocities committed on some of our wounded who had been captured, tortured and killed. Everyone of us who had so far survived, as well as our recently joined reinforcements, had become hardened both physically and mentally to the way of life. To kill any and every Japanese soldier was the aim, but to be taken prisoner, never! Endless marching, several major assaults and actions, frequent patrolling, the laying of ambushes, maintaining sentry duties, digging our trenches in every new area, burying our dead and evacuating our wounded, washing, cleaning our weapons and feeding ourselves; these were the daily necessities of life. Above all, we had to try to get enough sleep to keep us alert; two hours here, three hours there.

Before the monsoon broke in May, the temperature was in the eighties, with high humidity near the Irrawaddy river, on the plain. Flies and mosquitoes came to harry us as we buckled down to the 'new' street environment. We fought our way, step by step, through the remains of the bombed-out buildings, along the streets and roads in Mandalay City and its suburbs.

We found street fighting became very similar to that in the jungle. The noises were not quite so eerie but much else was of a similar mould. There was very limited visibility through and between the derelict buildings, with thick scrub along the street edges and among the piles of rubble, trees and bushes along the banks of the small dry rivulets and streams. By day, at corners and in the remains of the bazaar only recently abandoned, there were frequent opportunities

8. A clock tower in the western suburbs of Mandalay City, which was a landmark that survived until 1945. It was the site near the successful street ambushes of March 1945.

for surprise and unexpected encounters. By night, the crunch of feet on gravel or earth, lit only by half-seen moonlight and shadows, which were possibly imaginary, and between broken edifices, created a similar, uncertain environment. As always, every effort was made to ensure alertness and silence; to steal a march on our foes and inflict casualties by surprise.

To the accompaniment of the sounds of mortaring, shelling and small-arms fire, the remainder of our battalion were engaged in the final assault on Mandalay Hill, nearly two miles to the east. B Company was deployed to attack and hold Mandalay City, west of Fort Dufferin. This area remained in enemy occupation with much troop movement by day and night.

On 10 March, while outmanoeuvring and killing several Japanese rearguards, our men arrived at a major crossroads at the edge of the now deserted Zegyo bazaar. In the centre stood the solidly and tastefully constructed clock tower, almost undamaged, except for the marks of shell splinters. A landmark for both us and the enemy, a good opportunity was presented to lay an ambush. One or two enemy soldiers ran away after firing a few shots as our leading men approached. I decided that ambushes should be laid on the southern and western approaches by the main body of the company, while Sergeant Heywood and 6 Platoon moved to secure a crossroads further south. As night fell, it was apparent that small groups of Japanese were wandering about and trying to get into Fort Dufferin from the west, via the clock tower. The Fort lay some 600 yards to our east.

I had made it a key point of discipline that all movement should stop at nightfall. That afternoon, Corporal Arthur Pike of the Intelligence Section, guiding some of our administrative groups forward, arrived at last light. Now there could be no further movement, except by the enemy. If an emergency arose, those affected would have to shout the password if they needed to gain access to a position without being shot. Cool nerves were everywhere at a premium.

At about 8 p.m. on 10 March Private Stewart shot a lone figure within fifteen yards of his trench, sixty yards south of the clock tower. The omens looked good, but had he given the game away? At 10 p.m. there was still silence, except for the battle noises in the distance on Mandalay Hill. Was this enemy soldier entirely alone?

At 1 a.m. loud but indeterminate talking was heard to the southwest. Was it Japanese, Burmese, or could it be a British patrol from Sergeant Heywood's platoon in trouble? Decisions had to be taken. A wrong choice could lead to a disaster. Lance Corporal Paget, whose task was to give the signal by firing when enemy entered the ambush, coolly waited. Now chattering was heard. Clearly this group was the enemy. Lance Corporal Paget fired, as some twelve of them entered the killing area. Total surprise was achieved as the rest of the section joined in. Within minutes, a storm of grenades, small-arms fire and shouts and screams from the enemy told their own story. A few further shots were exchanged as the night wore on. Had we been successful?

Communication, other than by runners, was unavailable. However, runners could not move in the dark. At first light, the platoon commander and Lance Corporal Paget, together with Privates Stocks, Rainsford and Martin, searched the area. Private Stewart found that he had actually shot two enemy in front of his position, not just one, as he had thought. Elsewhere, the gory scenes near the clock tower unfolded. Eleven bodies were found. It seemed one of the enemy had blown himself up on his own grenade after being badly wounded. Hari-kiri, an honourable way out, had been taken by this Japanese soldier.

We had no casualties. The enemy dead included an officer complete with his ceremonial sword. Total success had been achieved. Private Stewart collected papers from the officer's pack for return to Company HQ and to be passed on for examination by the Intelligence Section. Private Rainsford passed the sword to Company HQ and Private Stocks achieved part of his goal to kill at least ten Japs to repay them for the death of his mate, Private Dodd, who had been killed earlier on 10 March.

This was an example of a successful outcome to a well-conceived ambush, in which there had been no loss to any of the ambushing group. Who deserved the credit? The answer is of course Lance Corporal Paget, Privates Stewart, Rainsford, Stocks, Martin and all the others in this group. Once again, discipline and patience had paid off. The enemy had again been destroyed as a result of the dedication and efficiency of our soldiers. But now it was 11 March and so the company moved on to the next operation to continue the defeat of our steadily deteriorating, but still ruthless opponents.

Before we moved from our clock tower base, one last patrol was sent out to find whether the Japanese were manning the south-west entrance and the walls of Fort Dufferin, some 600 yards to the east. Lance Corporal Paget, who by now had gained invaluable experience, volunteered to take the patrol with five men.

Around two hours later we heard machine-gun, rifle fire and grenade bursts from Lance Corporal Paget's direction. Then there was only silence. Paget had been told not to become heavily engaged. In another half hour of suspense for those of us around the clock tower, we saw the patrol returning with two men carrying a body. Our worst fears were realised. The patrol had been ambushed from the edge of the moat surrounding Fort Dufferin. The gate and the walls were defended strongly, but sadly Lance Corporal Paget, in gallantly returning fire on the enemy, had been killed by a single shot fired at close quarters. After a short but fierce engagement, the rest of the patrol extricated themselves, inflicting casualties on the enemy with no further loss to themselves. The price of obtaining information was the death of the exuberant and efficient Lance Corporal Paget, caught in an enemy ambush.

The term 'ambush' will loom long in the memories of those who fought in Burma through the heat and sweat in the jungles, on the plains and in the towns and villages as they fought their tough opponents.

9. A typical scene in the ruins of Mandalay City south of Fort Dufferin.

CHAPTER 4

'Spare the Pagodas'

There is a war on, a total war. It is a savage, down-to-earth, hand-to-hand conflict in a far-off country against a brutal, alien enemy. On one side, we were predominately Christian, Muslim or Hindu soldiers. Against us, the Japanese were almost exclusively Shintoists, a branch of Buddhism. All were operating in a land where Buddhism formed the background of religious observance. The local population was brought up to believe in suffering, and the way to release themselves from suffering, as a means of reaching nirvana, was complete subordination of the human spirit and character to a heavenly blissful state of existence. Religious beliefs, both those of the enemy and the Burmese, were important factors in planning our military operations.

In Burma, during peacetime, the Christian expatriate community had coexisted happily with the Buddhist population. The Colonial Government of Burma normally applied Christian principles in running the country. The traditional friendliness of the Burmese and of the hill tribes toward the British had been well established since the earlier Burma wars of the nineteenth century. In spite of the revolutionary party of Aung San, the Burmese co-operated with the Japanese to remove the 'colonial yoke'. Simmering below the surface, the nationalist feelings against being ruled by western people was beginning to affect the attitudes of local political parties toward the British Empire. The Japanese throughout the Far East were seizing opportunities to stir up local feelings against all of the former colonial powers. After the fall of Singapore in 1941, disaffected elements among Indian POWs were encouraged by them to join the so-called Indian National Army.

10. A chinthe, the mythological guardian of Burmese pagodas and monasteries.

Later, the Burma National Army took shape to work with the Japanese against the British with the promise of self government after the defeat of the British. Buddhism helped to cement these new alliances.

Most Allied soldiers were unaware of the niceties of the practical components of the religious divide or of the simmering political unrest. In many inhabited clearings in the jungles and in all the villages and small towns, as well as the main cities of Mandalay and Rangoon and along the great rivers, every area boasted at least one pagoda. The local people's total dedication to the worship of their Buddha is seen in the hundreds of dedicated, beautifully maintained, gold-covered edifices in religious centres, such as at Mandalay and Pagan, and at the central Shwedagon pagoda in Rangoon. This dedication is seen in the solitary pagoda, built usually of stone as a mark of respect, invariably sited on the eastern side of inhabited areas, including a few wooden huts, which often constituted a village.

Large, small, gold bedecked or just plain stone, pagodas became a factor in our lives. An edict had gone out to all Commonwealth Contingents in the 14th Army, 'Spare the Pagodas'. Our Army was not large. Our armaments were modest by modern standards, but the enemy was strong and ruthless. We needed as many 'plus points' on our side as possible. Why alienate a friendly local population by destroying their religious icons, unless truly unavoidable? As the Japanese had been known to use pagodas as part of their defensive positions, we, in contrast, could gain goodwill and obtain information about the enemy, as well as improve our reputation with the local people. Friendly Kachin, Karen, Shan and Chin tribesmen were already helping us. The Wingate expeditions of 1943 had received much assistance in guerrilla activities and in passing information about the enemy's movements. This assistance continued unabated for the undercover 'Force 136', providing guides and safe havens for our troops in the jungle areas and mountains. We would have been ill-advised to lose this help. 'Spare the Pagodas', therefore, made very good sense. A typical skirmish at Kin-U illustrates the point.

On 7 January 1945 4 Platoon, led by Lieutenant Charles Besly, led a charge through the wooden huts around the fences, now no longer holding cattle, over the Japanese bunker and foxhole defences. Close fire support from the mortars of the 33rd Anti-Tank Regiment and from our own mortars kept the enemy's heads down. No. 4 Platoon's objective was a line of three separate pagodas at the eastern side of the village, 600 yards from their start line. Smoke, explosions from grenades and the rattle of rifle and light machine-gun fire echoed everywhere. Enemy mortar bombs were now falling on our attacking troops as they penetrated the Japanese position with their objective, the three pagodas, well in sight.

As the skirmish developed, a steady stream of machine-gun fire sweeping the area came from the base of the pagoda on the left flank. No. 4 Platoon was forced to halt and then reduced to crawling forward, killing some eight enemy in the open by grenades and rifle fire. Gallantry and close support for each other had succeeded, as they finished off this close-quarter fighting with short bayonet charges. Behind them, grenade parties from Company HQ and the reserve section were neutralising the bunkers, from which the Japanese were now active. The initial surprise was over and 4 Platoon was unable to make further progress until the machine-gun fire from the pagoda on the left could be stopped. The firing was coming from the base of the building. By this time, Company HQ had moved forward to support the attack by 4 Platoon. It was almost incidental that we ran and crawled up to the steps of another pagoda in the village where we could now see and engage the enemy. So here we were taking cover from enemy fire on the steps of one pagoda, and at the same time engaging the enemy with small-arms fire into his position on another pagoda.

Should we bring our artillery support into action? Should we use our mortars on the building? Should we stay where we are? The answer to all these questions was 'Yes'. Not only could we now destroy the enemy position but also allow the attack to continue and save more of our men's lives by overcoming indecision. But it was also clear that the pagoda, from which the enemy was firing, would probably be destroyed, and also the one from where we were now firing would be damaged. Would this result in adverse publicity among the local population, when they returned? Would this action reduce information about the Japanese flowing in? And what might be the reaction of higher command to news of our disregard of the order to avoid damage to pagodas? To a soldier, the life of his mates, his own survival and the problems of immediate battle were foremost, rather than an obscure directive about religious icons. To us, the decision was simple – to press on, regardless.

At Company HQ, the company clerk Bill Lowe and company storeman Tom Stacey, both well-trained soldiers, were deployed under cover of the lowest pagoda steps. Ricochets continued to shower all those below with stones and masonry from the surrounding edifices. Crawling forward, intermittently firing shots at the enemy position, served to keep their heads down, while Tom Stacey, armed only with his rifle, coolly fired well-aimed shots into the Japanese machine-gun position. The fourth or fifth shot silenced this gun. Now, 4 Platoon was able to move forward again and rush the enemy still remaining around their pagoda. No artillery or mortar support was needed. No further enemy resistance was encountered. With the exuberant Tom Stacey, the small group from Company HQ was able to move off our pagoda steps to a more suitable defensive position as dusk fell, and with it Japanese resistance ceased.

This episode illustrates one of several unenviable choices that had to be made over and above local tactical requirements. Heat, dust, flies, mosquitoes and now religious undertones were to become an extra burden in dealing with our aggressive opponents. Perhaps the Buddha smiled down favourably on Tom Stacey, and on all of us as we left his temples intact. Nirvana may be our destiny also as the world moves on.

We now move to March 1945, to the southern suburbs of Mandalay. South of Fort Dufferin, B Company, supported by a troop of tanks, was closing in on some thirty or more Japanese who were holding derelict buildings on a piece of open, scrub-covered ground. At the centre of the buildings, a single gold-topped spire of a pagoda could clearly be seen flashing in the sun. Located in the area, the enemy was firing short-range 70mm and 75mm field guns into our positions and at our tanks. In response to cover our movements, our own field guns had engaged the enemy, carefully avoiding direct hits on the pagoda area, which was being bombed with smoke shells. Some twenty men of 6 Platoon, under their brave and resourceful platoon commander, Sergeant Heywood, moved forward by short bounds, closing in on the enemy position around the pagoda. Supported by four tanks firing steadily with their machine-guns to give covering fire, good progress was being made. Shouts from the Japanese, who could be seen moving in the pagoda area, enabled Privates Murray and Moore to shoot at least two of them.

Enemy machine-guns and a field gun were returning inaccurate fire, but still holding up the assault. Suddenly, a tank near the platoon commander took a direct hit from a shell into its engine and turret. Within seconds, the whole tank was ablaze, with its crew bailing out through the cupola, each more badly burnt than the next, falling onto the hard-packed earth and meeting their end as they struggled to extinguish the flames by rolling. Five men died in front of the attackers' eyes, but the drama was not yet over. Splinters and ricochets severely wounded Sergeant Heywood and two others as they moved forward, but the assault continued with renewed fury. With the throwing of grenades, firing machine-guns and with rifle and bayonet in use, the pagoda battle continued. To everyone's great sorrow, Sergeant Heywood was to die from his wounds, despite medical care, the next day, after a difficult evacuation under fire by stretcher bearers.

The niceties of preserving the pagoda were now forgotten. The enemy position was shelled with high explosives and, covered by machine-gun fire, the infantry assault overran the buildings, killing the few stragglers that remained, while the remainder of the enemy

11. The Shwedagon pagoda, Rangoon. Less ornate pagodas can be found all over Burma.

fled leaving two 70mm field guns in our hands. Unfortunately, the pagoda was almost totally destroyed by several direct hits. Japanese trenches were found around its feet. Which was the correct priority, saving the lives of men in 6 Platoon or preseving this religious icon? None of us had any doubts about the answer to that question.

12. A pagoda complex at Mandalay.

CHAPTER 5

Muddy Waters

Private Wells, a south countryman born in Kent, lay on his back chewing a long straw. Known as 'Ken', he was in fact Private Kenneth J. Wells of the Royal Berkshire Regiment, from Littlehampton, in Sussex. Of athletic build, he was sturdy with dark hair and eyes. His complexion had turned almost yellow from the daily dose of mepacrin, taken by everyone to prevent malaria.

Despite the noise of battle from the middle distance, Ken was in good humour this day, for he had just returned from a successful patrol led by his corporal with three other men and was enjoying a break for R & R (rest and relaxation). They had seen and reported on enemy activities some two miles away. Ken shot dead a Japanese sentry before the patrol withdrew with valuable information on the Jap position. Their skill and avoidance tactics had once again beaten the Japanese at their own game. It was 3 p.m. on 28 January 1945, a hot and windless day. The patrol had already brewed tea in their mess tins and had eaten some bully beef and biscuits. All were finding time for a well-earned sleep, lying in the shade under the scattered jungle and scrub that covered this defended area.

The next patrol, it was assumed, would be someone else's turn. He could run the chance of being shot or ambushed. Killing the enemy wherever possible would be measured against your own chances. This was Ken's main fear – ambush and counter ambush. He had experienced both. Now he was happy resting in the company area. He might even have time to write a letter home. There would be no more patrols for him, at least until tomorrow. They knew how easy it was to be shot

13. *The Irrawady River at Kabwet, 409 miles north of Mandalay. The Japanese bridgehead is on the west bank.*

up in this mobile infantry battle. Casualties were not easy to get back to base, which was miles away. If they were hit, they all knew the probabilities. Some of the non-smokers could smell the Japs before they got close to them, but nothing was certain. It was a mug's game searching the countryside in small reconnaissance patrols. Ken supposed it had to be done, but the information they usually got never seemed to add up to much. Two patrols of Japs, each of six men seen moving along a track, four Japs moving behind trees with rice bags on their heads, three Burmese crouching by a wooden hut smoking cheroots, the tracks of 70mm field guns, an enemy bivouac area with scattered debris and ammo boxes, and the well-known rubber Japanese boot soles of some twenty of the enemy imprinted in the dust . . . So the reports from his patrol leaders would go on, passed to the Company HQ and then to the Battalion Intelligence Section, and no doubt, further up the line for analysis and action.

The platoon sergeant would soon be round to inspect Ken's rifle. He thought he had better clean it or more guard duty would come his way. Why couldn't they trust him to clean it himself? If it jammed because of dirt, it meant his life, not theirs. As Ken sat up and got his pullthrough[*] out, he realised he had not yet dug his shelter trench. This was another irksome chore – a trench two feet deep and six feet long, shaped like a keyhole, which had to be dug every night with every new location. Two stray shells whistled over, reminding him of the need to dig the trench, but his sergeant seemed to think he wouldn't dig it if he was left to his own devices. They should have known that he needed no encouragement, having seen many casualties from enemy shelling. Pulling his rifle through and beginning to oil it, he noticed his entrenching tool, but with no enthusiasm. Just then, the platoon officer and sergeant came up to him. 'What had he done?', he wondered. 'Just going to dig down Sarge,' he announced guiltily, 'I've only just woken up, it won't take long.' Both his officer and sergeant looked serious. 'Wells,' said Lieutenant Whittingham-Jones, 'get dressed – you're on patrol again in an hour's time. Bring a submachine-gun and minimum equipment, including a water bottle. Be at platoon HQ in half an hour.' Incredulously, Ken heard the news. 'But I've only just got back Sarge,' he said. His platoon commander knew how Ken or any of them would feel. With so few men and so many commitments, routines had been upset before and this would happen again. This new mission was important. Ken was one of the best men he had. This was a patrol he, himself, would lead. 'Sorry Wells, but I've got to have you, we're going back to the area of your last patrol, I'll give you a break later.' Ken replied with a cheerful, 'Yes sir,' as he gave his pullthrough a savage tug up the barrel of his rifle. 'I'll come over Sir. Could someone dig my trench before we get back?' The sergeant looked hard at Ken. Sensing a battle of wills, the officer said, 'You won't need to dig tonight, we'll be moving off in the morning.' Ken breathed with relief. Ken's mate Crook whispered, 'good luck Kenny,' as they passed the last perimeter post. Each man carried a submachine-gun with two reserve magazines and two 36mm grenades on their belts. A water bottle slung over their shoulders and a field dressing in their pockets completed the picture.

Joining Lieutenant Whittingham-Jones half an hour later, Ken found Jimmy Seaby, the other member of the three-man reconnaissance patrol. Their orders made it clear that they were needed to go that

---

[*] A pullthrough is a metal weight at the end of a piece of cord, split at the end to hold a cotton square four inches by two inches with which all rifle barrels were cleaned. The patch, string and weight were pulled through the barrel to clean it. All riflemen carried pullthroughs.

night deep into the enemy's position. A close brush with the Japanese was in prospect. Behind them, they would leave the 'safety' of this position, opposite the main Japanese dug in defences. Just that day, 'Cushy'* Hudson, of another platoon, had been hit in the backside while digging his trench. He had been evacuated with considerable difficulty after being lifted, face down, onto a mule to make the rough, dangerous journey to the pick-up point where he could be loaded onto a Jeep. Shelling continued spasmodically. Ken and his patrol might even be in less danger on their patrol, away from the attention of the Jap artillery. Some hope, he thought.

Ahead of them, desultory exchanges of gun, machine-gun and rifle fire continued as their patrol commander gave them their orders:

> The position ahead is a Japanese beachhead on the west bank of the Irrawaddy, occupied by two battalions of the enemy. We are to move one and a half miles into the position, crawling through their outposts to report how many vehicles and of what type are in the position, and whether there are any tanks or armoured cars. The river will be on our right. There is no moon, so we must keep close together. I will lead, followed by Wells, then Seaby, three to five yards apart. There is to be no shooting, unless shot at. No other friendly patrols will be out. Speed and silence will give us our best chance. Enemy vehicles, if any, will be some 500 yards into the position. We start at 20:00 hours, so get some rest. If I get hit, our compass bearing is 120 degrees out and 240 back. The password is Muddy Waters. Time is now 16:30. Any questions?

Their return journey would be easier in the fading darkness before first light at about 4.30 a.m. Lieutenant Whittingham-Jones made both men realise that if the information was not obtained and reported to Company HQ by 5 a.m., they would have failed. They both returned to their sections to prepare themselves for another 'routine' patrol, to wash and reorganise their kit and weapons.

Still savouring his bully beef 'supper' and feeling refreshed by three mugs of extra-sweet tea, they made their way eastwards into the scrub and trees on the compass bearing 120°. The last glimmer of daylight was already turning into a dark grey, hot tropical night. Rising to his feet, the Lieutenant whispered, 'Another 200 yards, then we'll stop again.

---

* 'Cushy' derived from the Urdu word 'Dilkush' – a happy or cosy life, taking it easy. Corrupted by the Indians to Kushee, thence by the British to cushy.

Absolute silence. Ready, move.' Ken took a gulp from his water bottle. They crawled on.

His natural superstitions crept up on him and made him feel that this patrol might be more eventful than some. The orchestrated noises of the cicadas seemed louder than usual, as they passed the silhouette of a plantain tree with its dropping banana-shaped leaves, looking like a witch's fingers reaching down to them. He was almost surprised to get past, as they brushed his head and shoulders. Ken was number two in the patrol. Lieutenant Whittingham-Jones, with map case, compass and torch draped around his back, moved ahead with Jimmy Seaby some five yards behind him. Crawling, walking, pausing to find the way, they progressed slowly, if surely, pushing aside green lantana bushes and other fauna and flora which grew in abundance in their path. Moving parallel to the Irrawaddy river bank, some 200 yards from the river glinting in the hazy light, the noises of stray shots and muffled sound of shell fire ahead grew louder. The faintly seen tropical moon shone down, emphasising every shadow, decreasing the pace of their advance.

Now at some 1,000 yards from their starting point, they heard the clear sound of voices, short staccato sentences, both to their right by the river bank and ahead to their left. His platoon commander indicated their new direction between the two groups of voices. Jimmy Seaby closed up, now a yard apart, sweating profusely, crouching and crawling forward. They could hear both sets of voices to the right and left and the rattle of tin cans, probably mess tins. Japanese night discipline was not up to his company's standards and already their strange body smells pervaded the air. A beam of light, dim but distinctive, was shining down by the river, to their right. Now they had bypassed these voices, as they were obviously through the perimeter of the Jap positions. Still there was no sight of the enemy, but more noises were directly ahead. Lieutenant Whittingham-Jones halted and signalled that they should lie down. Noises and stray shots could be heard in front, then to their left, then behind them. No enemy movement could be seen. The air was tense with expectation for Ken, as they waited and listened, alert and sweating. Their mission had hardly begun. 'But where,' he thought, 'was the Jap transport they had been briefed to find there?' He was beginning to fear what lay ahead and all around.

Suddenly ahead, they heard an engine start up, with muffled metallic noises and urgent voices. Lieutenant Whittingham-Jones led them

14. The Irrawaddy river – the crossing secured.

to their left, circling around the enemy location. Two shadowy figures carrying bundles crossed in front. They dropped to the ground. Following the direction of these two enemy, they saw under the palm trees, just discernible in the dark, to left and right, the outline of some lorries with figures moving around them. Two vehicles were being loaded. Some others had their engines running. Waiting and watching, with hearts thumping for some ten minutes, which seemed like ten long hours to Ken, his Lieutenant whispered, 'no tanks, only six trucks. We'll head for home. Down to the river. They won't expect us from behind. Don't forget the password when we get back. What is it, Seaby?' 'Muddy Waters, sir,' came his muffled reply. Ken thought how easy to remember, as the Irrawaddy flowed past. So far their luck had held and now they were on their way back to report. Moving west on the new compass bearing, the river bank was now close on their left and an obvious landmark.

Suddenly it happened. At ten yards, a weird staccato challenge. Two shots from the flashes of the muzzles of two weapons ripped through the undergrowth past them. More voices were now shouting from where they had seen the transport. The three of them ran, bent low towards the river bank. Stumbling on, a fusillade of shots was directed at where they had been. Their cover was blown. To Ken's left a figure ran towards them. Ken emptied a full magazine from his submachine-gun into him as they jumped down the bank into the river. Japanese soldiers were running around like disturbed ants, as Ken's platoon commander fired at another Jap. Ken pulled the dead body out of his way and slung it into the river. Not the first dead Jap in the Irrawaddy, nor the last, he thought grimly. Below the bank, the three waded through waist-deep, black turgid water.

Against the skyline, as they moved through the water, several enemy were visible above them on the hillside by the bamboo thickets. To Ken's horror, he saw the beam of a torch shining down behind them onto the river. Surely they had been seen.

Were their worst fears about to be realised? The light beam some-how missed them but fixed itself where they had entered the river,

15. Private Kenneth J. Wells, aged twenty, proudly wearing the 19th Indian Division sign.

where Ken threw in the Jap body. To their astonishment, shots from every direction were fired at the corpse, which was barely visible. Again, Ken thought they had been seen. The cracks of several shots crossed their direction in the air as they scrambled on. Now a distant voice in broken English called out in the dark, 'Come here Johnny, come here Johnny,' as more shots fired behind them and into the river. Ken wondered where the Japs had learnt their English. Did they really expect a result? Stupid gits!

Lieutenant Whittingham-Jones, pausing as he urged them on through the murky water away from the voices, whispered, 'we're through – we've made it.' Of all the words Ken wanted to hear, none sounded more welcome. Two hundred yards further, stumbling out of the river and cautiously up the bank, they lay exhausted, recovering with sweet warm water from their bottles, listening to the shouts and crack and thump of bullets further back along the bank as the enemy attempted to find them. No Japs followed them.

Lieutenant Whittingham-Jones, Privates Wells and Seaby, maintaining cohesion and discipline, succeeded in their mission. Their skill in evading the enemy had been formidable. It only remained to cross the last 1,000 yards to their defended area in the dark before exchanging the password 'Muddy Waters' with an ever-alert sentry. Their stalwart platoon commander dismissed them with a laconic nod. 'Thanks, both of you, for a good night's work.' Their platoon sergeant seeing them return soaked to the skin, asked facetiously if they had enjoyed the swim! Ken began to clean his SMG (sub-machine gun). His sergeant said, 'Give it to me. We're off again in a few hours. Use Brown's slit trench if we get shelled. Get yourself some kip, you need it.' So his sergeant did care about him after all; not that Ken looked at it that way, but he appreciated the thought.

Another twenty-four hours in the life of Private K.J. Wells had passed. This time it was all in a night's work, he mused to himself. If he even thought about medals, he would have had in mind the old soldiers he had seen in India, proudly wearing their 'rooti gongs', originally awarded for eighteen years of Long Service and Good Conduct (LSGC). He and other wags knew they had really been awarded for 'long years of undetected crime', or so the saying went! One thing was sure – medals were not for young soldiers like him.

CHAPTER 6

'Die to the Last Man'

The dawn broke on a typically hot sunny morning. It was 6 a.m. on 29 January 1945. No. 6 Platoon of B Company, in their battle positions facing the Japanese-defended area at Kabwet, on the banks of the Irrawaddy river, began to 'stand down'. For an hour before first light, all had 'stood to' (full alert) in their battle positions. A well understood daily routine to avoid being surprised at one of the most likely times for the enemy to attack. Now sentries were again posted, food and water could be taken beside the foxholes, while final arrangements for the day's activities could be completed. A dawn patrol had reported 'enemy remain in occupation'. The usual gun and mortar fire, mixed with the crack and thump of stray rifle shots, had continued through the night.

No. 6 Platoon, having lost their commander by being wounded two weeks earlier, was now commanded by Sergeant Davies, a very experienced non-commissioned officer (NCO). During the night, one man had been wounded and was being evacuated. A stray shot had killed Sergeant Spicer of 4 Platoon the day before. In B Company, two men had been killed and fifteen wounded since arriving in the Kabwet area. Thus, the daily war of attrition continued unabated.

Today was to be the day. After much vital patrolling and harassment of the Japanese positions, sufficient information had been gained to make a full-scale assault. Some 200 of the enemy were now encircled with their backs to the Irrawaddy river on a 150 foot-high feature covered with trees, scrub and bamboo, 400 yards to our front, stretching for 1,000 yards along the hill and down to the river. Preliminary bombard-

16. The Irrawaddy river at the Kyaukmyaung crossing, forty miles north of Mandalay. Charles Wheeler, the BBC presenter, with the author visiting the crossing site for a VJ Memorial programme in 1995.

ment had softened up the enemy's defences along this ridge. Bunkers and foxholes had been accurately pinpointed. The main attack, with gunner and air support was to be launched at noon. Final preparations, such as bringing up reserve ammunition and rations, were now complete and final orders for the move forward and the assault were given by 10 a.m.

Sergeants Davies and Barrett were two of the platoon commanders who gathered their men together for a final briefing. This included a stiff reminder of the resistance likely to be encountered during the attack. Although all had taken part, both in reconnaissance and fighting patrols, this day was to see the first full-scale assault on a prepared and occupied Japanese defensive system by the battalion. B Company would lead the operation. Nothing less than total annihilation of the enemy would be acceptable. Every bunker, foxhole, thicket and scrub area would have to be cleared of the enemy.

Sergeant Davies reminded his men of the exhortations of Japanese generals, 'zenin yokugai' (die to the last man). This was more than just a piece of propaganda. The Emperor was, in their eyes, a god, to be worshipped from the heart by every Japanese soldier. No sacrifice was more praiseworthy or desirable than to die for the Emperor in any situation. Sergeant Davies and his men had heard stories of earlier battles against the Japanese in 1944. The stories of 'hari-kiri', or self-destruction, were passed down to all soldiers to steel them for the close-quarter battles which they now faced. They were told that as the enemy withdrew from their earlier defeats at Imphal and Kohima in 1944, the advancing 14th Army soldiers of the Durham Light Infantry, coming upon a desperately wounded Jap, heard him shout in broken English, 'give me a grenade to finish myself off'. In the same battalion in January 1945, in central Burma, while the British 2nd Division was overcoming an enemy position, a Japanese soldier had his rifle blown from his hands as he tried to defend himself. Surrender was not an option to him, as he physically assaulted the British company commander by sinking his teeth into his enemy's throat.

After their defeat at Kohima, the Japanese General Koturu openly regaled his troops to be prepared to die of starvation as they withdrew through Burma. Although beaten and retreating, such orders were accepted as part of a soldier's life in honouring and dying for his Emperor. Now with orders for the attack issued, Sergeant Davies and his men of 6 Platoon were ready to help each Jap they met to obey his general's order for the honour of the Emperor, 'to die to the last man'.

As the Hurribombers, Spitfires and gunner bombardments completed their tasks with mortars and machine-guns firing over head, 4 and 6 Platoons crossed the start line to cover the 400 yards to their objective, with the top of the hill to their front. In line, clambering, running and crouching, Privates Fabray and Baker soon found, in the dust of smoke and chaos of upturned earth, fallen trees and scrub debris, the bodies of three Japanese, dead in their positions. Baker saw the glint of a moving bayonet in a nearby foxhole. Firing from his hip, he scooped another Jap out of his hole. Alongside Baker, for a further twenty yards, came Crook, Dodd and Fabray, shooting into the bodies of the enemy, who were lying in the open, having attempted to run away. As several figures turned from their defences toward Lance Corporal Heath, he took the Bren gun and killed them. Two more of the enemy ran towards him as well, only to be mowed down.

All around the area, B Company men, bayonets fixed, were finishing off small pockets of the enemy who had survived the bombardment. The noise of small arms was deafening as the assault on the final Japanese positions succeeded in eliminating every defender. The lessons of the past were being followed. No enemy soldiers escaped from the position.

The count of Japanese dead and the search of their positions for weapons and documents now began. Corporal Arthur Pike and the Intelligence Section with the intelligence officer Captain Chris Simmons, began the laborious task of sifting through all the debris, clothes and equipment of every dead Japanese. Throughout all our operations, many down-to-earth practical differences became ever clearer between the Japanese way of life and ours. Whenever we had time to sift through the debris left by the enemy, new discoveries made us all realise how different our normal lives were from those of our enemy.

An example of this occurred when Private Downes pulled a small woolly doll, covered with small Japanese script, out of the pack of a dead Japanese. These were later identified as love poems. A strong offensive odour emanated from another pack. Private Baker opened the pack of the Japanese he had just killed and came to Company HQ carrying a packet of documents firmly attached to a bandaged, putrid hand severed at the wrist. It was well established that the Shinto religion required a part of a dead man's body to be taken back to the homeland and buried there. Such differences in national characteristics helped us to treat our enemy as they apparently wished to be treated, a race apart, helping us to steel our hearts against them.

It was at Kabwet that many bundles of Indian rupee notes, over-printed in Japanese, were also recovered. No doubt, all had been intended for the invasion of India – now useless to the retreating army but still, optimistically carried into battle.

A familiar sight after our Kabwet victories were the number of Japanese, rising sun miniature flags found on many dead soldiers. Perhaps this was a visual reminder to each man of his duty to die for his Emperor. Some of the larger flags found, carried prominently by officers or NCOs, were used by the enemy as rallying symbols when charging our positions. Nearly all had poems and exhortations printed on the silk material of which they were made. After perusal by the Intelligence Section, they provided interesting souvenirs for those who retained them.

Lance Corporal Lowe, the company clerk, with Privates Tuffs and Downes and the stretcher bearers, formed a firm base for Company HQ and its vital signallers, also helping to collect our own wounded for evacuation by Jeep ambulances manned by Americans attached to us from the American Volunteer Group organisation. Within the

17. The price of war. An unknown Japanese soldier who 'died to the last man'.

next twenty-four hours, the final remnants of the enemy withdrew across the river by night leaving the battalion in full control of the position. Before leaving the area, among other 'routines', promotion in the field to replace those NCOs who had been wounded or killed resulted in offers of promotion to Privates Ron Sibley and Ken Wells, both of whom deserved recognition for their dedicated and unselfish conduct.

Inevitably, losses had occurred. Sergeant Barrett, Corporal Bailey and Private Lea were killed, and Sergeants White, Edwards and Davies were wounded. The final tally of casualties was over ten to one, in our favour. The sad task of burying our dead in hastily dug graves was carried out before we left the area for further operations in the south.

General Bill Slim said in 1944 that 'there can be no question of the supreme courage and hardihood of the Japanese soldier. I know of no army that could have equalled them.' This statement, made by the foremost soldier in the Burma Campaign, speaks for itself and emphasises, if emphasis is needed, the philosophy of every Japanese soldier to 'die to the last man'.

CHAPTER 7

Eliminate the Machine-Gun in the Upstairs Room

It was nearly 4 p.m. on 7 March 1945 as B Company moved carefully forward, the leading men watching left to right, examining in turn, roofs, trees, doorways and windows as they moved steadily through the village of Madaya, about sixteen miles north of Mandalay. On the night before, in the marsh approaches to the village, Private W.H. Dale, our company runner, failed to return from a mission to make known the new password. Private Bill Vale, of 4 Platoon, reported that shortly after passing him, an exchange of rifle fire had been heard, followed by Japanese light machine-gun fire, then silence. In Appendix 2, Annex E, Private Dale is shown as 'missing' (see page 153). The true circumstances of his disappearance, and our loss of a valuable man, will sadly never be known.

Two earlier contact actions had revealed small groups of Japanese firing a few shots and running away, to repeat the process again, but each time with fewer men and in less well-organised parties. The main body of the battalion arrived in the centre of this straggling wooden-hutted village with its stone pagodas, all now apparently quiet and deserted. A number of stray chickens flapped and squawked across the dusty road. The air still smelt of smoke from the fires that had been used for cooking the day before. The CO decided that this village should be held for the night.

While plans were made and orders issued to confirm areas of responsibility, each platoon and company made systematic searches of the houses. A few resulting shots around the perimeter of the village showed that the enemy was still about. Near the edge of the market

18. A typical Burmese village house. Soldiers of 2nd Battalion take cover on the outskirts of Mandalay.

place, some 150 yards from the centre of the village, a two-storied wooden house stood gaunt and somewhat isolated from the others.

Sergeant Bob Scrivener and three men of B Company moved in to secure the house. Suddenly, the 'tap, tap, tap', the 'crack' and 'whine' of machine-gun fire came from the top floor. A small puff of oil smoke showed from the offending window. One man was hit, and some twenty officers and men who had collected round the CO for orders, flattened themselves, as ricochets and bullets ripped into the buildings and ground around them, throwing splinters, stones and dust at them as they crawled and scuttled quickly under cover at the edge of the village square. The CO's orders were postponed until later.

The village dogs made almost as much noise barking and complaining, while the small squad of gawky hens decided to flap and panic back over the road. Sergeant Scrivener and his three men were close to the house, but being unable to get into it, immediately engaged the enemy. One man moved to the back of the house but was held up by fire, for the Japs covered both ways. More firing followed from both windows. Two hand grenades were thrown, exploding harmlessly in the dusty square, while Sergeant Scrivener, close against the house wall, thought quickly how he could get at the enemy machine-gun (or guns) in the top room. He saw that the wooden stairs inside were open to the top storey. How many Japs were upstairs? If he rushed in, would he be met by a hail of fire? Both top windows were emitting spasmodic bursts of fire. Any movement in the market square was being engaged accurately. Two more men had been hit. It was clear that these Japs intended to lose their lives at a cost. While holding their fire and allowing the first troops to bypass them, there could be no escape. An area extending for over a mile around the centre of the village was held by some 500 British troops. With typical fanaticism, the enemy in this house had deliberately allowed themselves to be surrounded and were determined to fight it out in the hope of killing as many of their enemy as possible.

19. Entering Madaya from the west. Troops of the Royal Berkshire Regiment pass dead Japanese as they enter the town.

Sergeant Scrivener, crouching against the side of the house below the top room, had a problem on his hands. If he used phosphorous smoke grenades to hide their movements, the village would probably burn down right in the centre of the battalion area, for everything was tinder dry. If he ran from the house with his two men, they would be shot. If he entered the doorway and ran up the stairs, he risked being shot, as he would be silhouetted against the light timber frame of the house. So long as he remained against the house, no one else could engage the enemy without the risk of shooting him. Did the Japs know he was there and had they booby trapped the entrances?

Privates Jones and Smart were now alongside him. All three kept low, while the two distinct and different machine-guns continued their tap, tap, tapping in the room above. Each bout of firing made their gun bipods, standing on the timber floor, reverberate through the house, while the metallic chatter of empty cartridge cases, piling up on each other, could also be clearly heard. There seemed to be more than four men in the room, all talking excitedly. The boots of one man could be heard moving about the room, probably on look-out, Sergeant Scrivener thought, or possibly the leader of the group. He had experienced getting to close quarters with the enemy before, but never had such a bizarre situation faced him. Fire and move-ment with rifle and machine-gun under normal circumstances, the one giving cover fire while the others moved, would have presented no problem. He had learned street-fighting techniques but here was a new situation, to root out an enemy without being free to deploy even such small fire power that he and his two men possessed, for fear of hitting other men of the unit who were scattered around the square. If only the Japanese were like the Germans, or better still, the Italians, then they might surrender if he fired up into the top of the house and called on them to come out. As the firing continued, Sergeant Scrivener moved silently and quickly around the building to find out if it would be possible to climb to the second floor. Jones and Smart crouched against the wall, ready to shoot instantly should any Jap show his head through a window. Now they were once again joined by Sergeant Scrivener. The sergeant had made up his mind. Here was his plan:

> Jones, you stay watching the stair exit. If they come down, let'em have it. Use your rifle only, no grenades or you may damage yourself as well. Smart, you're coming with me to that corner of the building. When I give

the signal, you open rapid fire at the open window. I'm going to the rear and will throw a grenade through the open window. Then under your cover fire I'll rush them up the stairs. There's no way up, bar the stairs. We'll take a chance it's not booby trapped or mined. Stop firing when I throw a smoke grenade out of the window, and join me fast. If I'm shot, the smoke will help cover you, then you will have to shoot it out.

'Yes, Sarge,' they replied. They both understood the risks – four Japs, two machine-guns, a rickety open staircase, possibly booby trapped, and a crazy sergeant. If he wanted to do it his way, that was his affair. For their part, they hoped he would succeed. If not, they'd have to do it themselves. But hadn't they already seen enough men die?

Their progress was now being watched by many men from the neighbouring buildings around the square. Smart, following close behind Sergeant Scrivener, hugging the edge of the house, moved swiftly to his corner. Sergeant Scrivener pointed to a pile of timber about three feet from the wall. 'Into that, lad, and open up when you're ready; steady bursts, but keep firing to drown my noise,' he ordered. Turning, he started to return to Jones back at the entrance. Noticing that the guns in the upstairs room were no longer firing, he glanced upwards. As he did so, he was just in time to see a Jap grenade coming down towards him. He threw himself to the ground, the grenade bounced on the hard, caked earth some twelve feet from him and, thinking he was about to be hit, shielding his head, he waited for the inevitable. Looking up, he saw that the grenade failed to explode. 'Some people are born lucky,' he thought. At the same time, from behind him, Smart's gun began to pour a steady stream of shots into the back window of the room above. In a flash, Sergeant Scrivener was on his feet. Storming past Jones, he cleared the first eight stairs in two bounds, turned, and was lost to sight on the landing. The onlookers heard two sharp explosions. Dust and smoke wisped out of the windows. The sharp crack and thump of Smart's gun was now complemented by the short staccato bursts of a Sten submachine-gun, two further Sten bursts . . . then silence! A phosphorous grenade suddenly threw a puff of white smoke across the square. Sergeant Scrivener's voice shouted, 'Cease fire, stop firing,' and a tousled head appeared at the window of the upstairs room. 'Jones, join me here. Smart, remain in position,' he shouted to the two men. It was clear that the opposition had been overcome. A search of the house would now follow and the routines of the unit preparing for the night's operation could begin.

Two men from Company HQ moved quickly to douse the phosphorous grenade, still spluttering below the house.

Later, upstairs, the intelligence officer, moving in to search for identification, found four dead Japanese, two machine-guns, four rifles and enough ammunition to supply a company, stacked neatly in cartons round the walls. Cooking pots and clothing disclosed that the occupants had been here for some two days, and judging by the feathers some of the village hens had justification for their panic! These four Japanese, although they were cut off and surrounded, had decided to die for their Emperor in battle – the highest honour sought by Japanese soldiers. Inspired by their cause, they dearly sold their lives. Sergeant Scrivener, in foiling their intentions, had seen to it that their only victims were three men wounded. His first two grenades killed two Japs and stunned the others. His Sten gun had successfully eliminated the remaining two before they could recover from his onslaught.

Another man had shown that to risk one's life in an assault and to court death in the interests of others was the only way the enemy could be defeated. Sergeant Scrivener would simply have said, if he had been asked, that it was all part of a day's work. 'Get the brew going, lads' was his only comment on rejoining the rest of his platoon.

CHAPTER 8

Saving the Perimeter

A young Berkshireman, five feet five inches tall and eighteen years of age, conscripted into the Army, reported to the Regimental Depot in Reading, in 1940. These barracks were named after the famous Guernsey-born soldier, General Sir Isaac Brock, who had saved Canada from the little remembered American invasion between 1812 and 1814. General Brock commanded the 49th Foot, which was to become the Royal Berkshire Regiment. Now, some 130 years later, this young Berkshireman, as with generations of soldiers of the regiment, would have Brock Barracks indelibly inscribed on his memory, with early training days at the heart of his regiment. Developing his physique, enlarging his knowledge and building on an enthusiastic approach to soldiering, Private Ronald Godley soon showed his potential.

Drafted to the 6th Battalion of the regiment in 1941, Ron Godley grew in stature, ability and strength. Promoted to Lance Corporal in 1943, he was posted to the 2nd Battalion of the regiment, then in Madras, India, in early 1944. Training for jungle warfare through the monsoon and tropical heat, young Ron, by then twenty-five, made his mark on those around him as a first-class rifle shot, good at games and with high marks from various training courses he had attended. He was soon promoted to full corporal, and at the conclusion of the battalion's jungle training for Burma, was further promoted to sergeant in late 1944. Ron Godley served, with distinction, in all of his battalion's early engagements from December 1944 to March 1945, surviving both shot and shell during the advance against the enemy.

20. *Preparing a typical section of the perimeter defences in Mandalay.*

21. *The General Officer Commanding 19th Indian (Dagger) Division – Major General T.W. Rees – standing on the walls of Fort Dufferin after its capture on 20 March 1945, with some of his staff officers.*

In the absence of officer reinforcements, in March 1945, Ron Godley was made acting platoon commander of 5 Platoon, now reduced from its normal strength of thirty-six to only nineteen NCOs and men. Attrition had taken its toll on the platoon – the number of soldiers killed and wounded had been high. During the 200-mile advance from the Indian border to the great city of Mandalay, Godley and his platoon had been engaged in endless patrol contacts, five major actions and a number of running battles with the retreating enemy. Godley and his platoon had learnt much about the Japanese soldier, his habits, tactics and his bravery. One thing stood out, Godley and his men knew they were more a match for the enemy. Even the fabled ability of the Japanese to move about by night and to set cleverly concealed ambushes did not disturb him. He could, and would outsmart them whatever the circumstances. Often careless and noisy, the Japanese sometimes gave themselves away and paid the penalty.

The battle for Mandalay Hill and in the city had lasted two weeks. Two weeks of continuous movement and fighting occurred in the streets north-west, west and south-west of its citadel, Fort Dufferin. A trickle of reinforcements had kept Godley's platoon at a strength of some twenty-two men. The battle for Mandalay Hill, in which the other half of the battalion was engaged, had taken five days. Gurkhas, Baluchis, Sikhs and the Frontier Force Rifles, their Indian Army comrades, were all part of the jigsaw, smashing down Japanese defences, down, supported by the gunners and sappers, and fighter and bomber aircraft.

Both C and D Companies had greatly distinguished themselves on the Hill, while A Company and Godley's own B Company were assaulting the city west of Fort Dufferin.

Night and day, the onslaught continued. Heat and dust, mosquitoes and flies added to the rigours of the slow but determined advance through the debris and chaos of ramshackle brick and wooden houses littering their path. Japanese rearguards, local defence posts and scattered strong points were methodically overcome. Godley and his men were sometimes involved in a set-piece company attack, supported by mortars and guns, sometimes doing their own thing in surrounding, neutralising and overrunning these last-ditch Japanese posts, using their own LMGs[*] and mortars for cover fire. Among many successful patrol actions, Lieutenant Whittingham-Jones with four men,

---

[*]   Light machine-guns.

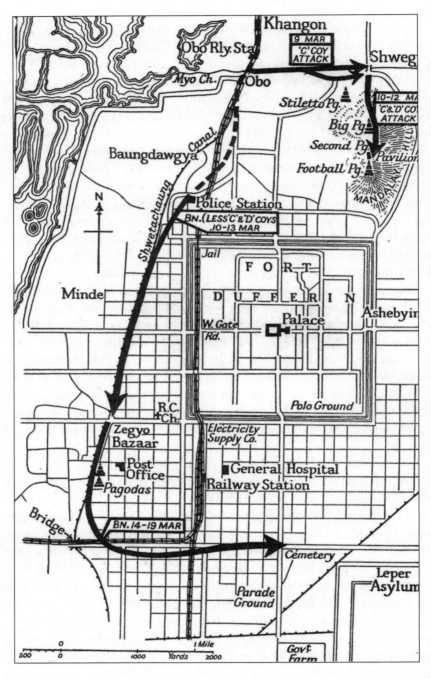

22. *Mandalay, 1945.*

23. Members of 2nd Batallion commence the attack on Mandalay Hill.

including Private R. Tully, using 2ft mortars and grenades, fought their way around an enemy outpost, killing all three occupants. By 18 March the formidable Fort Dufferin, with its 30ft-thick, 10ft-high walls and surrounded by a 30ft-wide moat full of water, was being assaulted from the north and east by other units of the 19th Indian Division. By then Godley and his company were south of Fort Dufferin, hemming in large numbers of the enemy, while the final battering continued. Their task now was to kill as many enemy as possible, should they decide to escape southwards. Deployed as part of a stop line, forming a perimeter some 600 yards from Fort Dufferin's walls, he sited two sections about twenty yards apart, dug in, while he and his third section entrenched themselves in the rear where he could best give cover fire and control the situation as it developed.

On 18 March Godley had patrolled forward to the Fort's walls, meeting and engaging the usual small groups of Japanese, noticeably some were now infiltrating away from the Fort to the south. Intelligence reported that a breakout from the Fort was soon likely. Other divisional infantry, attacking from the north and east, continued to assault across the moat. Heavy bombardment by guns and mortars, now commonplace to Godley, continued night and day, with ricochets and stray shells falling around them, but still the defenders held the Fort. It had already survived the onslaught for some fourteen days. Japanese casualties, both inside and outside the Fort's walls, were high by any standards. No. 5 Platoon alone had killed several small groups in the city streets. As a result of one of Godley's earlier successful reconnaissance patrols, valuable information had been obtained alerting the battalion to an imminent breakout. For this and earlier good work Godley had been recommended for a bravery award, but this had not yet been gazetted. On the night of 18 March, two parties of the enemy, larger than usual, ran into his platoon's defended posts. Six men had been killed, with the remainder running past shouting to each other as they went. Three of his men had been hit by grenade splinters. With the trenches being necessarily widely spaced out, it was impossible to prevent some enemy getting through the positions on this scattered perimeter. He had laid his defence out, covering the two main streets in the area to block the enemy's most likely routes.

Now it was the evening of 19 March. Godley's men were weary, thirsty, hot and busy. Plenty of water had been brought up, and their 'K' rations supplied first-grade snacks and vitamins to keep them going. He grimly compared this with that of the enemy's situation of water shortage, no meat and only poor-quality rice. Also, what of their casualties? They had no advanced dressing stations nor casualty clearing stations. So they could expect nothing but total suffering and endless pain. It was no wonder they wanted to die for their Emperor. His most recent casualties had already been successfully evacuated by Jeep to Company HQ and, no doubt, were now being treated effectively down the casevac (casualty evacuation scheme) 'chain'. Deploying over the area of streets and broken-down huts covered in debris, Godley's company commander had been up to see him. He in turn visited all his section posts along the perimeter of the company area, reminding his men that the Jap resistance in the Fort might soon crumble and more enemy would be likely to come south that night. Alertness was essential. Every dead Jap would mean fewer to fight later as the battle moved on. Booby traps and improvised wire obstacles between sections needed strengthening. Fields of fire needed checking. By dusk all was still. Sentries were posted, passwords rehearsed and mepacrin pills taken to avoid the dreaded malaria. The noise of firing to the north continued. Stray bullets cracked their way over their heads. Sleep had become a matter of discipline. Sentries on stag knew their responsibilities, while the rest fell into a fitful sleep – even two or three hours helped them regain their strength.

It was 2 a.m. Desultory noises of battle continued to be heard when Godley and his men were alerted by the sentries. In the dark, figures had been seen and voices heard urgently talking – the platoon 'stood-to' in their shallow trenches. Now the right-hand section's LMG fired two long bursts into the darkness. Shouts and screams rent the air less than 100 yards away. All over the area, the enemy was moving in on them. Godley could see them stumbling and running towards them. Realising that their own spasmodic rifle and machine-gun fire was not enough to stop them, two bodies had already fallen some ten yards out, he and his runner leapt from their trench with SMG and rifle firing from the hip as they stood spraying the area to their front. The screaming enemy came on. The whole platoon was now in action. Godley shouted, 'Keep them out,' and had the satisfaction of seeing the Japs to his immediate front fall in the grey darkness. The night was illuminated by explosions. The noise of screams, shouts and groanings from some of the Japs on the ground told him they were losing their impetus. A small group of three charged towards him. He emptied his second magazine into them. His runner finished off one with his rifle butt. All along his platoon area the noise was dying down. Were they gathering for another attack? After an hour he shouted to his three section commanders by name. They replied that all was well. Two casualties remained to be evacuated in the morning. All of them could hear enemy movement to the south. None came near for the rest of the night. As dawn broke, Godley sent out a patrol. Eleven more Japanese bodies were counted in front of the position and two beside their defences. The battle along the company's area of the perimeter was over. He and his men had survived another night full of action, but by now the enemy had had enough. On 20 March the Fort was reported clear of the enemy. Those that survived bypassed them through the gaps in the perimeter elsewhere, taking with them neither vehicles nor animals and abandoning all their supplies and ammunition. They must have been in very poor shape and would not get far. Ron Godley and his platoon had inflicted grave losses on the enemy. Their part of the perimeter had been saved from being overrun. They could now have a short respite before pursuing the enemy to the south.

Still no enemy tried to give themselves up, despite the dropping of leaflets by the RAF offering them incentives to do so. The larger of these leaflets reminded them of the parlous state in which the Japanese nation, both across the Pacific and near their homeland, now found herself, with defeats at Iwo Jima, Luzon and the Philippines. Extracts from leaflets dropped in March 1945 follow. At first, the leaflets attempted to soften up their soldiers, with the main illustration presenting a calm scene from their homeland and Japanese script reading, 'In the evening, after a day's journey, I decided to sleep under the cherry tree. Then the cherry blossom is the landlord for tonight.'

Then followed news items that reported sightings of B29 bombers over their children at home, and the devastation on their industrial areas from the bombing of their homeland. Closer to those soldiers in Burma, they described the failure of the Japanese command to prevent continued retreat and loss of life, their inability to stop Mandalay and Rangoon from being retaken was made clear. They said their 'lifeline' (supply line) had been cut by the Allies and they could not recieve medical provisions or ammunition, unlike the 'huge planes' of the Allies which were able to bring in arms, ammunition and supplies to the front-line troops regardless of weight. Japanese casualties were listed in all their theatres by numbers, of which 55,000 in Burma were highlighted.

All of these leaflets fell in the areas of the beaten and retreating Japanese for maximum effect. In a reference to the failure to defend the homeland and all the losses being sustained close to Japan and in their cities, a paragraph of a leaflet read, 'according to the military rulers it is for the country to die in any battlefield, but if the homeland is not defended securely it must be quite nonsense to die on a battlefield far away from home, mustn't it?' At the foot of the leaflet is written, 'The bearer of this leaflet wants to surrender, please keep him under your protection.' How many of the men of B Company or in Ron Godley's platoon ever found a Japanese soldier carrying one of these leaflets to offer surrender is an open question. You will not be surprised to learn that although leaflets were found in Japanese positions, not one single soldier ever surrendered.

A translation of a second leaflet dropped by the RAF, also in March 1945, specifically for the Burma theatre, is reproduced in Appendix 1, Annex B. Its main purpose was to undermine the Japanese soldier's confidence and trust in his commanders. The strength of the Japanese ethos of dying for the Emperor remained intact, despite the continued misery of defeat and the death of so many of their comrades at the hands of Sergeant Ron Godley and his group of Slim's Burma Boys.

24. *A news leaflet dropped by the RAF informing the Japanese of the world situation.*

Did Ron Godley deserve another medal so soon after the recommendations already submitted for his earlier action? Of course he did! But other matters were taking priority. He and his men received orders to move in transport around the north of Mandalay to form another perimeter some forty miles south to catch the enemy as they tried to break out of our cordons. There was more essential work for all to do in disorganising the Japanese withdrawal and keeping them on the run.

CHAPTER 9

'Expect the Unexpected'

The road to Mawchi, a town high in the eastern mountains separating Burma from Thailand, runs from the central rail, river and road routes through Burma. Starting at the significant town of Toungoo, some 170 miles north of Rangoon (Yangon), the road crosses higher reaches of the Sittang river, winding its way through jungle and scrub up the steep escarpments known as 'the staircase', because of its many twists and turns. For some four miles east of the town, the road crosses a low-lying area adjacent to the Sittang river before beginning its climb to the distant mountains. At the four-mile point, a low range of hills, rising some 300 feet above the surrounding country, dominates the ancient town of Toungoo and the eastern approaches to it. Astride this road, the first operation was made in April 1945 to cut off one of the main Japanese escape routes into Thailand.

The battalion, after its successes on the road to Mandalay, in the city itself and on the roads south to Toungoo, was now given the task of clearing the Japanese from the town and then pursuing them up the only road through the jungles and hills, some thousands of feet up to Mawchi. They had organised strong rearguards along this mountainous escape route out of Burma. Determined well-armed enemy infantry barred the way over ground, which gave the defence every advantage.

Enemy shelling from field guns in the foothills and scattered Japanese patrols were causing casualties to administrative and other support troops in and around the town. The first task was to clear the immediate area around Toungoo and seize the dominating ridges along the hills, four miles away. The removal of enemy OPs[*] and rearguards could prepare the base for the closure of this escape route to Japanese forces now withdrawing from west to east across Burma.

In B Company, only forty men of the original 120 who crossed the border into Burma in November 1944 survived. These survivors had covered 400 miles in four months of bruising campaigning, covering at first the same ground as that taken by the first Wingate expedition in 1943, from Tonhe to Pinlebu, and from Wuntho, Kyaikthin and Kin-U down the central railway corridor. Turning east over the Irrawaddy river at Singu, they had battled for three weeks at Kabwet on the Irrawaddy bank to reach the town of Madaya and into Mandalay. After its capture, a short break at Maymyo to reorganise allowed the absorption of reinforcements to undergo urgent training and rebuild B Company once again into an effective fighting force.

Sixteen weeks of continuous campaigning, with endless patrolling and skirmishes, including three major actions, had taken their toll. Thirty-five men had been killed or died of wounds and sixty-seven battle casualties had been evacuated. Desultory enemy shelling had caused casualties, but in the main it was the daily and nightly close-quarter battles with rifle, submachine-gun, light machine-gun, grenade and bayonet that created the greatest damage to life and limb. The enemy, forced on the defensive everywhere, lost heavily in these engagements. The journey through Burma was hazardous in the extreme, none more so than on the Mawchi road, east of Toungoo. As our soldiers discovered, no Japanese would ever surrender. Most died where they fought. Each action for them was a fight to the death, the ultimate glory for all Japanese soldiers, which increased the hazards for the attacker.

On the morning of 28 April 1945 the Japanese defences, astride the main road, prevented the battalion from advancing. B Company was given the task of carrying out a right-flanking move to bypass the enemy on the road, seizing part of the range of hills two miles to the south and then moving north to cut the road behind the Japanese position along the ridge. Gathering a section of three-inch mortars to give us close support, we realised that the eight mules, which normally carried the mortars and our reserve ammunition and water, had not yet caught up with us, having had to march every step of the way. The rest of us had been brought some of the way south in three-ton

---

[*] Observation Posts

lorries. The mules, with their muleteers, including Privates Buckle and Bagwell, were several days march away. One hundred men in a long winding column on a compass bearing, now began the move out into the open scrub and jungle. All the three-inch mortar barrels and base plates, weighing half a hundredweight, had to be man handled. The thirty-six bombs, each weighing 10lb, and all the company's reserve ammunition, had to be distributed to riflemen already carrying their own packs, arms and other equipment. Food and water for three days were shared out. Because it was carrying extra loads, this column was only able to move very slowly.

Twenty-five per cent of the men at the head of the column had to be ready for immediate action. Their packs were therefore redistributed among the rest of the column. 'Expect the unexpected and not just the enemy' was the watchword. Extra burdens, for as long as required, had to be accepted by all. Cheerful and ribald remarks greeted those with heavier or bulky loads, especially from some of the smaller men, some of whom were about five foot tall. Cheerful banter was returned, with interest, when reliefs took place during this move.

So we set off through enemy gunfire at the edge of Toungoo. We slowly plodded through the scrub at first, along broken flat ground in line ahead formation, disappearing into six-foot high 'Kuna' grass. The map showed a blank space, giving no indication that we were entering a marsh. There was no way round, so we stumbled on to negotiate a row of hummocks which rose through the grass. There was no sign of the enemy. It was quickly apparent that the hummocks were the home of great white ants, as the leading elements found to their cost. A halt was called to allow those at the front to extricate themselves and remove this new 'enemy'. Had a Japanese post been near, he would have seen several soldiers stripped bare to get rid of the ants that had tried to hold us up. 'Whatever next?' Laboriously slow, with halts every few yards, we crept on through the clogging marshy terrain. No fate would be worse than to be caught strung out in this defenceless ground. Slowly, but surely, dragging our feet out of the mire, we moved on.

Our plan to seize a foothold on the top of the ridge towering some 300 feet above us was now urgent. Immersed in jungle, we needed to climb up and then deploy along the top. The leading platoon deploying to the right and left, leaving their large packs and any reserve ammunition to be carried as extra burdens by the other two platoons. At the foot of the hill, we waited for the signal to advance – a white vest waved on a stick – and to our relief, seeing the sign after half an hour, the rest of us slowly pulled themselves up to the top. The temperature was in the eighties and the air was more humid than usual, caused by the moist air over the marsh. Searching the area disclosed signs of enemy activity. Their well-known rubber sole footprints were discovered, as well as Japanese ammunition boxes and wrappings, but no enemy. With two cases of heat stroke and in an exhausted state, an NCO and two men were sent two miles along the ridge towards the road to report on any enemy activity. We now halted for the night. No enemy were found by this patrol.

At dawn, the advance along the ridge continued towards the road. Within an hour first contact was made – as usual, near a pagoda. Corporal Ron Sibley and his section chased away a small group of the enemy who ran away towards the road. By midday, our advance was halted again. Sergeant Chalky White reported an enemy defensive position some 200 yards wide, astride the route of our advance.

The heat and mosquitoes seemed to be on the side of the Japanese as we halted to probe forward and prepare for an assault. The stretcher bearers had already recovered four cases of heatstroke, returning via the marsh to Toungoo. We now engaged the Japanese position with small arms and mortar fire, while patrols from each platoon were dispatched to discover the extent of the enemy position and his strength. Most water bottles needed replenishment to avoid the risk of dehydration. Parties were organised to refill them from the marsh. Each man carried a sterilising kit of twenty pills. All would now be able to take on another twenty-four hours worth of water. Rations for four days had been distributed. These were bully beef and biscuits, with a few boxes of American 'K' rations.

Later that day, the CO came through on the radio with an order to halt our movement for twenty-four hours, while C and D Companies closed up. The Japanese were still able to shell Toungoo, so it was vital to attack and clear them off the ridge. On the morning of the fourth day after further patrolling and visits to the marsh for water, C and D Companies had arrived and a co-ordinated attack on the enemy position was planned. B Company, supported by our own mortars, was to attack the southern end of the ridge to the front, while the remainder of the battalion moved against the northern end astride the Mawchi road. The enemy had now become more active. Their shelling and small-arms fire continued to keep heads down as the final preparations were made.

B Company attacked with two platoons at 10 a.m. on the fourth day. No further food or ammunition, nor supporting fire was available but time was now of the essence. However, throughout our moves and actions in the jungle, the undergrowth had been a major obstacle, especially in secondary jungle where trees had been felled and the area replanted. Each man carried a dah to cut his way through. Here on the hillside, in open scrub, we could see that lentana bushes grew in profusion along the ridge between the trees. This wiry twisting shrub, more suitable to Kew Gardens greenhouses than here, caused impediments to movement wherever it grew. Luckily, we had so far not been impeded, but dahs were out as we prepared for the attack through the bamboo and lentana wilderness.

Within three hours, we had assaulted the pagoda area and followed along the ridge to another, and joined forces with C and D Companies on the Mawchi road. Fifteen of the enemy had been killed by our skilful fire and movement, and individual assaults followed closely behind the three-inch mortar fire support. Twenty of the enemy were seen running away. Some were cut down as they ran. B Company casualties saw two killed, including Private Adkins, who had been with us since the earliest training days in India. Among the three wounded, one man had been shot through the stomach. Holding himself together, doubled up, he was placed on a stretcher and within two hours was in medical hands to recover completely from a grievous, life-threatening wound. Bravery and skill were evident everywhere. Each section of six men worked together, with the light machine-gunner engaging the Japanese foxhole positions while the riflemen assaulted. The usual shouts and screams of the enemy became almost laughable to those who had chased them through the country, for they now gave their positions away making it easier to pinpoint them. The monsoon broke overnight just before the final assault and everyone was completely soaked, lying in the water with only light ponchos for cover.

The usual problems of tactical decision making now loomed large. The elements had turned against us, but risks still had to be taken and decisions made. Should we postpone the attack until we could more easily operate and see our way? Not likely! Now was the time for the Japanese to expect the unexpected. The Japanese might have thought 'they won't attack yet'. How wrong they were, as they found to their cost, on this and many similar occasions. Our men defied the monsoon and all the odds to do their duty, right up to the final days of the war on the precipitous Mawchi road to Thailand in August 1945.

25. East of Toungoo – near the Mawchi Road.

As the rains poured down, patrols were organised to follow up the retreating Japanese. Ken Wells, who had rejoined the company after a severe bout of dysentery, was leading scout of one patrol, easing its way through the jungle fringes on each side of the road. Cautiously probing forward, moving slowly in short bounds, Wells spotted smoke rising some 200 yards ahead. Was it a Burmese village or a Jap encampment? Ken whispered to his corporal, 'look, there they are.' 'They' were a small group of soldiers. Their helmets and long rifles could only be those of the enemy. Ken and his corporal had to make sure that this indistinct group were indeed Japanese, for the Indian and Gurkha battalions were now moving wide around their flanks and might have strayed onto the Mawchi road ahead. No mistakes could be made.

How many Japs were there? Crawling closer, it now became clear that the patrol had come upon an unsuspecting enemy group. No sentries could be seen and the smoke came from a fire under a cooking pot with some six men crouching round it. What an opportunity this was. Quickly briefing his men, the corporal deployed the patrol and charged into the enemy group, supported by their own light machine-gun fire. Ken Wells killed one man as he turned to fire, and in his own words said, 'we really caught them with their pants down. There were no survivors.' In the firefight, some ten Japanese were killed, with no loss to the patrol – a rare opportunity brilliantly seized. This enemy group was so obviously demoralised by the weather and jungle conditions that, abandoning their own security, they stopped to rest and dry off. A wild pig was cooking in the pot. In their packs scores of bundles of Japanese overprinted rupee notes were found.

Ken and his patrol triumphantly returned to their base ready for the next move forward up the road. The rain teemed down but without respite. B Company moved on again: 'expect the unexpected.' No one had any doubts that more surprises would be in store for them as they continued the advance, astride the road in jungle formation towards Mawchi. Duty must be done, despite tactical hazards and relentless monsoon.

CHAPTER 10

'They also Serve who only Stand and Wait'

In the spring of 1945, some 750,000 British, Indian and Allied ground forces were operating in South-East Asia. Of this number, some 30 per cent were infantry and an additional 10 per cent were supporting arms, such as gunners, tanks, field engineers, signallers and staff. Thus 60 per cent of the total figure represented the huge administrative tail needed to back up, maintain and supply the forward troops. Infantry units also included their own integral administrative elements to maintain the chain of supply right into the front line. It will come as no surprise to learn that of out of all those killed or wounded in action, 90 per cent were infantrymen and their supporting arms. In the air, a similar imbalance existed between fighter and bomber aircrew on the one hand, and administrative or ground staff on the other.

The majority of our men were between twenty and twenty-four years of age, and most were wartime conscripts. While realising the essential need for backup units to provide administrative support, most did not see that support as a part of the real world in which they lived, which, put briefly, was the world of kill or be killed. This was a world where, at any time, savage wounds might send a man to the hospital, perhaps never to return. The real world was where skill and cunning could not only preserve one's life but also reduce the enemy's fighting strength; man by man, as each Japanese position was shelled, shot at and assaulted, until only mangled and dead bodies, weary soldiers and the debris of war remained. This was B Company's war. No one was arrogant, but our combat mentality was reinforced as the campaign continued, with strong feelings of losing friends and comrades seldom experienced in the rear areas. But those in the infantry and their close supporting arms, would never have agreed to exchange their role for any 'cushy number' at the back.

The Air Forces

From the moment that B Company entered Burma in December 1944 two or three times a week the steady presence of Dakota supply aircraft could be seen and heard behind and over us as we moved through the jungles, over the Chindwin river and onto the central plains. These planes were a morale raiser for all. From mid-January to May 1945, as the tempo of operations increased, the frequency and volume of supply by air also stepped up to almost daily sorties, with regular parachute drops bringing in all of our requirements. Free-falling drops of straw and grain for our mules could also be seen being despatched through the cargo doors, the dispatchers waving to us as they watched the bundles dropping and bouncing behind our positions.

From time to time, the dropping zones (DZ) were quite close, per-haps 600 yards behind our positions. One day, 28 February 1945, B Company provided a collection party on the DZ to collect the drop and pass it to men from the rear echelon. Three Dakotas circled the area and soon bundles of supplies for all of us and our mules were descend-ing onto the scrub and tree-covered ground. One of our Berkshiremen, Company Quartermaster Sergeant Freed sat in his Jeep with his driver, Private Hellyer, under a tree, checking the drop near the edge of the DZ. To the horror of onlookers, a free-dropped bale of straw fell through the trees hitting Freed and Hellyer, killing both of them outright. Here two of our administrative helpers, who ought to have been safe, were no less vulnerable than our riflemen.

A month earlier, while we were still in the jungle, we had our eyes opened to the hazards of flying in support of ground forces. In the heat of a tropical evening, we watched from our defensive positions on the fringe of a jungle clearing, four Japanese Zero fighters circle the sky above us. Unknown to the Japanese pilots and also to us, a supply drop was due in the area. Just as the Zeros seemed to be flying off, we heard the roar of our larger aircraft approaching. Perhaps we would now see an air battle overhead but no, the aircraft approaching were of course an unescorted group of Dakotas, which began to drop their loads on the nearby DZ. Apparently unaware of the danger in the sky, these Dakotas suddenly found all hell breaking out around them. In no time, despite trying to take avoiding action, each of the five aircraft had been shot down. The Zeros rose before each attack and descended like cats pouncing on a mouse. The Dakotas had no chance, crashing into the jungle, where a black ball of smoke indicated their destruction. The RASC (Royal Army Service Corps) dispatchers were seen at the cargo door of one aircraft, desperately jumping as their aircraft skimmed the tops of the trees. Sadly, there were no survivors. All the crews perished as the Japanese pilots flashed their wings and disappeared to the south.

Air supply in Burma reached a peak in 1945, unequalled in volume in any other theatre of war. The C47 Dakotas flew an average of three sorties each day, and between January and March 1945 delivered a total of 250,000 tons of stores. Both the Dakotas and the light Air OP Auster aircraft landed on make-shift, forward airstrips to evacuate casualties from the casualty clearing stations five to ten miles behind the forward area. The Austers operated close behind the infantry, evacuating casualties, as well as providing eyes in the sky for our gunners to pinpoint enemy targets and carry out accurate shoots controlled by these pilots.

By the end of February 1945 the Japanese air effort had virtually ceased, thanks to complete air supremacy gained by the sorties of our B25 bombers operating from airfields in India and destroying their bases in south Burma, Malaya and Thailand.

All of us in B Company had personal experience of the close support provided by fighter aircraft Hurribombers, Spitfires and B25 bombers as we closed in on Mandalay. No one who was there will ever forget the massive air support directed onto our targets, first at Kabwet on the Irrawaddy river, forty miles north of the city, and then at Mandalay City itself. B25 bombers arrived from their bases in India, hundreds of miles distant, to launch their 1,000lb bombs onto one small hill feature, removing most of the hillside in which the Japanese were entrenched, all in split-second timing, co-ordinated with B Company's attack and with the overhead cover by the Sikh machine-gunners. The Hurribombers and Spitfires continued sweeping the enemy positions. The roar of engines was immense and the morale of the attacking soldiers at its peak. Sergeant Spicer of 5 Platoon took back all he had rudely said about 'the Brylcreme Boys'. Accuracy, persistence and effective neutralisation of the enemy positions were huge rewards for those assaulting the defences. Back at their bases, the RAF and USAAF airmen probably never knew how much we valued their efforts.

26. Dropping supplies in the hills east of the Chindwin river . . .

27. . . . near Shwebo, west of the Irrawaddy river . . .

28. . . . and on the plains near Kabwet.

Military Support

In the 14th Army, there were 72,000 engineers and 130,000 labour-ers from India working on the infrastructure, including making or improving roads and bridges, providing boats and assistance at river crossings and lifting enemy mines. Those of us in the infantry owed much to the efficiency and dedication to sometimes mundane tasks of the Royal Engineers and Indian Pioneers. We had good reason to be grateful to them and to realise that they were just as vulnerable to Japanese shelling as we were. Working in the river and marsh areas and down in the valleys, perhaps they were even more vulnerable to the mosquitoes, ticks, flies and poor air quality which pervaded all the habitats in which they had to live and work.

Stretcher bearers, south of Mandalay, not normally expected to act as riflemen in an assault or defence, found themselves filling this role when numbers of men in sections were reduced. Reverting to their normal tasks, indefatigably, they looked after the wounded until they could be evacuated by Jeep down the long casualty evacuation chain. This was from the regimental aid post to the advanced dressing station, then on to the main dressing station and finally to the casualty clearing station.

So many of our men owed their lives to the skill of the medical officers and their staff – 'they also serve . . .' Some service too! On 25 April
in the jungle-clad hills east of Wundwin, the stretcher bearers with
B Company were wounded by shell fire while preparing to dress other
wounded men. In turn, they themselves had to be evacuated.

In 1945 the manpower required to maintain signal communications
was significant. A shortage of radio sets resulted in many signallers
not only manning defences in the front area, but also carrying out the
physical laying of cables across 'impossible' terrain to maintain contact
by field telephone, often under enemy observation and shelling.

Routinely, the food and stores chain, controlled at the battalion level
by our ever-present quartermaster, Captain Monty Sumray, and his
staff, was our vital link with the necessities of life in the field to keep
us going, separated as we were, hundreds of miles from India, by land
or air.

The front end of the food chain was epitomised by the mule team of
B Company, led by Lance Corporal Rollinson, with Privates Bagwell
and Buckle in this group of eight. They marched every yard of the
way from the Indian border, keeping their mules in good health, while
enduring small arms and gun fire as they arrived in the forward positions with their precious loads of ammunition, water and other vital
stores. How much was owed to these stalwart animals and their brave
muleteers? Shelled, mortared and fired on, they were indispensable.
Behind our own muleteers came the second echelons, part of the Royal
Indian Army Service Corps (RIASC), manned by Indian soldiers. They
were ubiquitous, and many joined us in our battle areas.

Unusually, almost up at the sharp end as the battle moved south,
after the clearance of Mandalay and at Toungoo, came mobile bath
units and ENSA groups. These were morale boosters for those off duty
but were sometimes within enemy shelling range. The Tully brothers,
who were competent accordion players, remember the 'Ted and Jock'
accordion team, who accompanied the sing-songs as they established
themselves in the so-called rest areas during the few breaks they
enjoyed.

Finally, men from many other arms and services, organised by
the Divisional and Brigade Staff, found themselves serving with
B Company alongside our riflemen, from time to time. B Company
could not have done without them. Many a soldier had cause to
thank this host of supporters for their individual and collective efforts
throughout the campaign.

29. The Maiwand Lion in Forbury Gardens, Reading, Berkshire. The Memorial to 285 Officers and Men of the 66th Berkshire Regiment, who were killed at Maiwand in Afghanistan, 27 July 1880.

30. Soldiers of the 2nd Battalion with captured Japanese weapons at the end of the war.

'They also serve who only stand and wait.' This quotation from Milton's sonnet may apply to many who in fact did so much more than serve, in risking their lives to help keep the infantry at the sharp end sharp.

In the Forbury Gardens, Reading, Berkshire, there is a memorial to 285 officers and men of the 66th Berkshire Regiment, who were killed at Maiwand in Afghanistan on 27 July 1880. The epitaph reads, 'History does not afford any grander or finer instance of gallantry and devotion to Queen and Country than that displayed by the 66th Regiment on 27 July 1880.'

The 66th Regiment were the forebears of the Royal Berkshire Regiment, whose 2nd Battalion bore the number 66. The Royal Berkshire Regiment has been amalgamated with the Wiltshire Regiment and, in 1994 the Gloucestershire Regiment was to form the new Royal Gloucestershire, Berkshire and Wiltshire Regiment.

It is one of the outstanding pieces of history which acted as an inspiration and spur to those who served in Burma in the Second World War.

CHAPTER 11

Unfinished Business

On a sunny Sunday morning in January 1945 some sixty men of B Company were resting out of action in the scrub country north-east of the town of Shwebo, in the central Burma plains. In these three weeks of action, we had been in almost continuous hand-to-hand battles and skirmishes with the retreating Japanese rearguards. We had killed, and counted, thirty-five enemy dead. Our own losses had been nine men killed and fourteen wounded. We had crossed the Chindwin river into Burma with a ninety-strong contingent of officers and other ranks. Ninety British wartime warriors, in for the duration of the war, had trained for both the jungle and open warfare, and life in the tropics, for two years or more across India. We were prepared to give our all for 'King and Country' as history would dictate and duty required.

Our 'baptism of fire' had seen one third of our men killed or wounded. Weak in numbers but confident in our military skills and strong in spirit, we now had time to reflect on our performance and to prepare urgently the few reinforcements we were now receiving for the next stage of our operations.

We remembered past regimental achievements, none more so than the Battle of Maiwand in 1880. Our predecessors, the 66th (Berkshire) Regiment, had fought in similar primitive conditions in Afghanistan. To put it mildly, they had not let the side down, and nor would we. Their inspiration lived on in Burma.

'Get your waterwings on,' a visiting staff officer from the 19th Indian Division HQ guardedly whispered to us. His coded message needed no imagination for us to guess that this meant the assault crossing of the 1,500-yard wide Irrawaddy river, flowing fast some ten miles to our east. Another trial of strength and character for us lay ahead.

In these three days of our 'rest', we had time to clean and repair arms and equipment, to wash clothes and ourselves thoroughly, to check and replenish ammunition, reserve rations and medical stores, and to receive and write letters home. All of this was in between refresher training periods, the routine posting of sentries and the practising of 'stand to' in our shallow trenches to avoid the risk of being surprised by enemy patrols in the area.

At the start of operations, our baggage train, which included blankets and bedrolls, had been left behind at our base near Imphal, to be brought forward by stages as opportunities arise. In our peacetime training, similar periods without our bedding usually lasted for less than a week. No such luxury as the welcome comfort of a blanket was possible here for weeks on end. Priorities for our load-carrying mules and Jeeps were strictly ammunition, wireless batteries, water, food and medical supplies. There was no space for blankets. Sleeping in our battledress, heads pillowed on our large packs, we lay among the jungle crawlies on the dusty earth or, on fleeting occasions, on the floor of wooden Burmese shacks. Hardened we may have become, but the simple delight of wrapping oneself in an Army blanket when it did arrive on later occasions, was a distinct morale booster. They were a reminder of the good things in life out of action, and our belief in a better future.

Both now, and for a similar short three-day break after the recapture of Mandalay, we found essential time for drill parades taken by Company Sergeant Major Savage. In the chaotic living conditions of battle, a return to 'old fashioned' ideals of discipline on a parade ground helped a feeling of normality and cohesion. On the flat, hard-baked paddy fields, the standard of drill was far from perfect, but striving for perfection under Company Sergeant Major Savage's eagle eyes gave all a morale boost and helped to integrate the latest reinforcements with the older hands.

Alongside all these practical activities, we also found that we had some unfinished business. Our mental and psychological attitudes to several aspects of the all-out war in which we were engaged were brought home to us in these first three weeks of our trials by fire, topics seldom realistically discussed or practised, yet of fundamental importance to soldiers alone or in small groups on the battlefield. The longer we remained in action over the ensuing months, the more the topics discussed were confirmed as motivators and factors of significance in our lives – such as religious beliefs, of our own and of the enemy, burying our dead comrades and the enemy, attitudes toward killing and to prisoners, by both sides and tending our wounded comrades during action.

Other topics were just as significant, such as the performance of our gallant American Volunteer Group. They were attached to us to drive Jeep ambulances and succour our wounded in battle. Nearly all were conscientious objectors to carrying and using arms or were unfit for military service.

The effects of failure to carry out orders in action also served as a motivator, as did the penalties for cowardice in the face of the enemy, niceties of the law, 'when on active service' and the practical meaning of morale.

These situations and the questions they posed were, of course, at the back of most soldiers' minds. Few liked to confront some of these topics, preferring to treat them as ongoing, uncomfortable or unfinished business. It was important in the total commitment to our task and to each other that the subjects should be properly aired, for they all had a strong bearing on morale, one of the most important principles of war.

Attempts at satisfactory explanations and logical thought patterns undoubtedly helped men through the stress of battle. Some preferred to ignore the subjects altogether, if possible, but for the great majority they offered a valuable psychological safety net, an extra bulwark against the otherwise mind-sapping daily events surrounding infantry soldiers in action. It should be remembered that our average age was in the early twenties, not an age when unproved theories or inexact doctrines are readily accepted, even when they are understood.

Religious Beliefs

In the Army, before and early in the war, church parades were held weekly. No excuses for absence were accepted. This routine was maintained until joining the battle area in November 1944. For the great majority, religious beliefs were based on the Anglican traditional services, as laid down in the Book of Common Prayer. Practising Roman Catholics were permitted to attend separate services. Now the Christian way of life was to be tested severely. Did we soldiers really believe in Christ as the Saviour of the world? Did we believe in saying our prayers? Did we look for spiritual support in acknowledging our human failings? How did we reconcile the loss of a comrade and friend in battle with the mercy of God? Perhaps our long traditions did help us to recognise that, in war, life itself was a constant lottery for survival.

As the crump of bursting shells and crackle of machine-gun fire surged around our positions, causing casualties, more questions needed answers. Were we, as Christians, helped and sustained by our beliefs? If the worst happened, did we believe that a better life awaited us in the next world? Each man was on his own with his thoughts. No longer were the routines of church parades there to give moral support. Fear, that great demoraliser, had to be conquered. We needed beliefs to get us through our trials in battle. Belief in our cause, in our leaders, in our training and tactical efficiency, belief in our way of life and in our ability to beat the Japanese, carried us through.

31. *Maymyo parish church. Men of the 2nd Battalion the Royal Berkshire Regiment leaving the first service at the church after its recapture in March 1945 – faith renewed.*

From Christmas Day 1944 our regimental chaplain's personal example gave us reassurance that Christian beliefs mattered. At every engagement, and afterwards, Padre Barry was to be seen comforting those who were wounded and ministering to the dying. A small ,slightly built man, moving about unarmed, he became a symbol of religious stability for all to see. Without his presence, even those who held strong religious beliefs would have found life harder to bear when shot and shell were taking their toll. When forming up for attacks, with all the uncertainties around us, he was a living reminder that we were Christian soldiers. A huge contrast existed between our attitudes and those of the enemy, which were based on their Shinto religion. The best and worst examples were illustrated by the treatment of each others' casualties and of the dead. After each engagement, and as at Kin-U, our own dead were buried quietly in marked graves after a short service, attended by those of us who were not immediately engaged elsewhere. Some ten enemy soldiers in that battle were also laid to rest in a communal grave after a short service given by Padre Barry. Records of Japanese behaviour to our dead in similar circumstances showed a callous disregard for such religious niceties. Mass, unmarked graves were the best that could be expected.

Attitudes to Killing

'Thou shalt do no murder' is one of the Ten Commandments. It is a basic tenet of Christian teaching. How did we reconcile this commandment with our fundamental aim to kill every Japanese soldier we met in combat? Was this murder? Murdering or killing, could we be expected to understand the difference? How many even thought of the Ten Commandments and their application to us as soldiers? Some may have considered the Scriptures but accepted that we had practical work to do. Had we not sung lustily and often in our church services 'Onward Christian soldiers marching as to war . . .', and 'Soldiers of Christ arise and put your armour on . . .'? This was a full acceptance by the Church of the existence of the 'just war' and our involvement in it.

These hymns are based on the teachings of St Paul. from the first century AD. His letter to the Ephesians was one of a number of exhortations to encourage and help people of his day to believe in Jesus Christ, as the Son of God. 'Take up God's armour; then you will be able to stand your ground when things are at their worst, to complete every task and still to stand. Stand firm I say.' In the Psalms of David, further exhortations to believe in the Lord God Almighty included reminders of His help to the Israelites as they escaped the disasters of their days. 'Who remembered us when we were in trouble . . . and hath delivered us from our enemies . . . for His mercy endureth forever.' Few of us would have absorbed these teachings at the time, but they lay behind our Christian upbringing, helping Padre Barry to enable us to 'stand firm' whatever the circumstances.

We were attempting to stop an unlawful invasion of a land of peaceful people, working to earn their living in part of the British Empire. The Japanese had decided to take on the might of the United States and Great Britain. Right was on our side. The Japanese could expect no mercy until they were beaten and their government forced to sue for peace. In God's eyes, we were surely to be exonerated, despite our total dedication to kill fellow human beings. An earlier version of our Prayer Book read, 'Thou shalt not kill.' This was later changed to 'Thou shalt do no murder.' For those who considered these things it was refreshing to believe that 'murder' was classed as illegal killing while we were supported by the law in our actions against the enemy, even when it resulted in his death. Our Christian teachings exposed this apparent anomaly, but this explanation seemed to resolve the mental conflict satisfactorily for those who thought about it. But who does think about it? Far away from the battle area, death in action is a deplorable thought, something to which a nation, family and friends must be resigned but at arm's length from personal life. Even those within the combat zones in Burma were seldom required to experience shot and shell, unless they were in direct close quarters with the enemy. So it was at the infantry level and in their supporting elements, mainly gunners, tank crews, medium machine-gunners and sappers, that 'killing' took on a day-to-day realism in the infantry, more so than in any other arm of the service, close-quarter fighting, often hand-to-hand, brought the true realities of war to life. Casualties came, not from long-distance air bombardment, nor from gun barrages, but from direct small-arms fire. Here, out in the open, Padre Barry talked and encouraged us, 'pray for forgiveness and help in all you do'. The Padre remained unprotected at his own risk, yet was always up with our forward elements. His faith in God was apparent wherever he went.

In contrast to our belief in Christian values, the Japanese attitude to killing was governed by their Shinto beliefs and Samurai traditions. To die in battle for the Emperor was the greatest honour for every soldier. If a Japanese position was being overrun, they knew they should kill themselves rather than surrender. A Japanese soldier taken prisoner was considered by their high command as being no longer 'alive' – he would never be accepted back into main-stream Japanese society. He should therefore be dispatched into the next world. Hari-kiri was thus common throughout their services. As in other areas of Burma and the Far East, Allied prisoners were given no mercy. Wounded British soldiers, who had been captured at Kabwet, were found to have been mistreated and killed. In marked contrast, when we took a Japanese prisoner alive near Mandalay, he was treated strictly under the terms of the Geneva Convention.

In more recent days, the Emperor of Japan's renewed apologies for the mistreatment of POWs on the Burma Railway and elsewhere has raised much public interest. The plight of those individuals who suffered brutality, hardship and torture at Japanese hands, all well established and documented, has again been aired with a view to financial compensation from the Japanese government. Attempts have been made to equate German, Russian and Yugoslav treatment of POWs with those of the Japanese as an emollient to Japanese feelings. There can be no such equation. By factual evidence, the cruelty and treatment of prisoners of war by the Japanese was without equal, anywhere in the wartime world. Those few POWs who still survive, almost all in ill-health and now in their eighties and nineties, deserve the fullest possible compensation for their unspeakable and uniquely cruel treatment. No political or other consideration should prevent such practical action by the Japanese. However, many apologies may be offered by their Emperor. It is surprising that Allied governments, from countries whose citizens suffered indescribable hardship at the hands of the Japanese, should not have fought harder on their behalf. This includes our own government, whatever its political persuasion.

Attitudes to Wounded Comrades in Action

Battle drills are taught in training to help eliminate uncertainties when shot and shell are flying around on the battlefield, and to provide routine movements and precise actions so as to enable soldiers to concentrate on the job at hand, helping to overcome fear and the often chaotic conditions surrounding them.

On peaceful training exercises, from time to time, the simulation of casualties was practised. 'Killing off' some of the participants usually resulted, unsurprisingly, in chaos and confusion. Exercise directors, with limited time to teach many important tactical lessons, tended to prevent the umpires from creating too many deaths, especially among the officers and NCOs. The real-life casualties and events we had experienced, especially at Kin-U and Kabwet, had brought this aspect of soldiering sharply into focus. The bonding of our battle teams, whether three, seven or twenty men, ensured a cohesion and fellow-ship in which each knew his place in the organisation with resulting maximum efficiency.

As we looked back on our first few weeks in which several had been killed or wounded, it was apparent that natural human reaction was taking its toll. We saw comrades being hit; those who had one minute been running or crawling forward, now shattered with flowing blood and torn clothing, were crumpled on the ground writhing and shout-ing in pain. All were close to those who were unharmed. How many times had we inculcated the principle that the attack must be main-tained at all costs? No succour for the wounded was permitted: 'leave them to the stretcher bearers; press on until the objective is reached.' In defence, in a two-man team on a light machine-gun, the gun must continue to be manned and fired as part of the tactical plan. To tend to a wounded comrade when one of the team was hit meant a silent gun and no support for others, who relied on its fire power to support an assault or hold off enemy attacks. No first aid could be given until the tactical situation permitted it. This was an absolute imperative, but how difficult it was in practice to maintain when one was a severely wounded friend, struck down by a bullet or shell splinter.

These real-life dramas had to be seriously faced. No text book could offer a solution, but the difficult human principle to first defeat the enemy then succour the wounded had to be thoroughly understood. Compromises could weaken our resolve. A tendency to stop and tend to the wounded could not be accepted. The wounded had to be pre-pared to wait their turn until the battle moved on and help could be given. This was much easier said than done, but the lessons were impressed on all and had to be obeyed. First aid would be given as soon as practicable, with self help a priority using individual first field dressings.

Our Gallant American Volunteer Group
Jeep Drivers and Medical Assistants

B Company was supported by a Jeep ambulance with two stretchers mounted on top, manned by two Americans from a small group
of assistants attached to our battalion. Usually, the same two men
were with us, but sometimes the team was increased, according to
circumstances.

Our two Americans typified our view of the Yanks, as we knew
them. They were laconic, gum-chewing and, in today's parlance, laid-
back men, until we needed their very real skills. Sharing their 'K'
rations and water with those nearest to them, usually in Company HQ,
their steely worth became admired and understood.

They tended the wounded, then evacuated them on the Jeep stretchers to Battalion HQ five or six miles away, sometimes at night along
dirt paths and tracks open to ambush by the Japanese, to return for
more as soon as possible. They were morale boosters in those days
of continual movement, when the casevac system ended hundreds
of miles to the rear as the advance continued. In the main these men
were American conscientious objectors and those unfit for military
service. Compulsorily drafted to Burma by their government, they
were unarmed but always willing and able to aid the wounded and
dying. Their dedication to their tasks was total. Many of them were
highly intelligent, educated individuals. Their self doubts about killing, often based on religious scruples, had given them greater courage
to buck the system and face opprobrium at home. John Parkhurst,
from Boston, Massachusetts, was one of these outstanding Americans
attached to B Company.

During our three weeks of daily and nightly attrition at Kabwet, both
in our defensive position and in the series of attacks on the Japanese
position, our American medics were in action taking our wounded to
the regimental Aid Post at Battalion HQ, often under cover of darkness. At Company HQ, our stretcher bearers, led by Corporal Pettit,
were able to pass their wounded charges on to the Americans. At
Kabwet, Sergeant Edwards received a severe wound in his legs, and
assisted by Lance Corporal Bill Lowe, he was evacuated by stretcher
to the American's Jeep. Sergeant Edwards was a strong man of some
fourteen stone. We had benefited from the valuable experience of his
days with the Chindits. His departure was sadly missed, not only for
his efficiency, but also for his boisterous good humour and aggressive

attitude towards the enemy. He was a morale booster for all around him. The arguments for and against conscientious objectors in time of national emergency are too numerous and complex to discuss here. However, for the genuine protester, his courage and tenacity in the face of ridicule, scorn and open opposition from his erstwhile friends deserved a medal.

The Effects of Failure to Carry out Orders in Action and Cowardice in the Face of the Enemy

Time had moved on. Our philosophising at Shwebo about the more nebulous side of soldiering had led, over the weeks, to a realisation that the root and branch of successes we were experiencing, not only stemmed from our disciplinary routines, but also from the hand of fate itself. Those of us who survived through the daily actions at Kin-U, at Kabwet, on the west bank of the Irrawaddy, down the long marches interlaced with skirmishes, through Madaya to Mandalay and then on to Toungoo, Zeyawadi and up the Mawchi road, seldom had time for personal reflection. Why had we lost so many comrades? Why had we come through this far?

At Maymo, after the long days and nights of attrition and bloodshed at Mandalay, where we had our second brief respite, we had time to look back and realise that Padre Barry was right. He had advised us to 'Trust in God and let the devil take the hindmost'. The discipline of the church parade was restored as we all attended the parish church for the first service after the Japanese had been evicted. It was a cheerful and reflective occasion. It was a time to refresh ourselves before the next call on our resources, and to relearn old lessons, sort out our weaknesses and develop our strengths.

Weaknesses – did we have any at this time of euphoria when so many tasks had tested our abilities and skills? We had suffered grievous losses in NCOs and platoon commanders, our junior leaders. All had been replaced from within the company. We were now down to only forty-five men, from the sixty which had remained a month ago at Shwebo. For our survivors, the foundations for refusing to obey orders from our recently promoted, very young and inexperienced NCOs, and of failing to carry out their instructions, leading to cowardice in the face of the enemy, were now classically in place. It was normal practice, after casualties had weakened the skill and ability of battle-torn units, for refitting and relief to take place. Reinforcements, particularly of commanders at all levels, would arrive and the routines of the battlefield within units would be restored – but this took time and time was not on our side.

Despite every difficulty in maintaining ourselves in action effectively after NCOs had been killed or wounded and when our sections had been reduced to two or three men, often widely scattered and lightly supported within their platoons; despite thirst, heat and constant fear, no signs were evident of any failure to 'press on regardless'. Confidence remained high with all those who had been recently promoted, supporting and being supported by their men.

Throughout a soldier's service, behind all his activities stands his oath of allegiance to the Crown and, as in any worthwhile walk of life, a set of rules and laws are established to support an organised efficient society and to govern conduct.

The Manual of Military Law under the Army Act gave us the guidance for our behaviour in every circumstance. The law was administered under this authority by the regiment or by the other officers appointed from neighbouring units from the British or Indian Army. Offences committed, 'Whilst on Active Service', were considered to be more serious than similar crimes in peacetime situations. In the field, those who transgressed could be punished, either summarily in their own unit or remanded for a trial by court martial.

Minor misdemeanours of soldiers in an infantry battalion occurred from time to time, but few soldiers failed to realise that disciplinary errors were unacceptable in battle conditions which could affect everyone's lives. Company Sergeant Major Staples, and later after his death, Company Sergeant Major Savage, and in turn, his successor, were able to offer practical advice and caution to would-be transgressors to bring them to their senses before the formal processes of law had to be invoked. In action, recourse to the formal legal process was thus extremely rare.

In B Company that did not mean that admonitions were never needed, such as to maintain water discipline when it was scarce, swallow the daily mepacrin tablet to suppress malaria, care for and clean personal arms and equipment, shave and wash both body and clothes whenever possible. The admonitions to use foot powder to reduce foot rot, avoid smoking cigarettes or lighting fires when close to the enemy, dig personal protection trenches and latrines when halted for any appreciable period, remain fully alert when posted as a sentry, and to seize the opportunity to sleep whenever possible at short halts and rests were to be heeded as well. The mundane task of burying debris after meals to avoid giving away our movements and strengths was another important chore when enemy patrols were around. All the disciplinary routines made sense to everyone but, not unsurprisingly, needed to be made very clear to new reinforcements. Cheerful banter and good spirits made these enforced restrictions easier to accept.

In similar circumstances elsewhere, we read of near or actual mutinies. We had realised that to keep your head down when the enemy was firing at you might save your life even if your mates might suffer. Cowardice was an easy way out, unless you were very unlucky to be seen. Temptations were for the weakhearted, the selfish and for those who had failed to understand there could be no relaxation from duty, no excuses.

Cowardice in the face of the enemy, for whatever reason, abject fear, inadequacy or battle stress can spread like an infection in the chaos of a battle. This insidious human reaction requires firm control wherever it is found if military forces are not to disintegrate. Skill, discipline and *esprit de corps* had to be maintained at all costs, whatever the prevailing conditions. As we found in Burma, the priority given in peace-time training to these three aspects of soldiering was the foundation for our effectiveness in war. Our reliance on the *Military Law* was the last sanction to be used.

The Practical Meaning of Morale

That much overworked word 'morale', one of the most important principles of war, sums up, in practice, at an infantry soldier's level what he needs to keep going through each twenty-four hours, day and night, in monsoon rain or parched humidity. Sometimes he is without food and water. He may be dirty, unkempt and weary, yet willing and able to maintain the momentum, proud to serve among his friends and colleagues many thousands of miles away from his homeland.

Much has already been written about the essential training and combat preparation to produce a technically superior and physically fit soldier, but behind all the operational necessities lies the heart and soul of the man. No matter how efficient, without confidence-boosting backup all will fail when under pressure, with uncertainties and fear making their presence felt in every new situation, undermining all the training and skill built into a soldier's operational effectiveness. Confidence in the leadership, the adequate supply of all things to keep a man fed and watered, and the knowledge that the medics are ready when required, all help to maintain morale.

However, two very personal matters are of importance, family and friends. These two aspects of life become even more important for a soldier, who is far away from home in an unfriendly environment. Letters to and from home have a special impact on the goodwill, enthusiasm and cheerful acceptance of hardship in war. Contact with family, whenever reasonably possible, is so much part of a soldier's life and should have high priority in a well-run unit.

Secondly, the bonds which link men, often from very different backgrounds, education and experiences, are a vital ingredient when campaigning in far-away lands, such as Burma. Regimental *esprit de corps*, based on stirring aspects of the regiment's history, and the cohesion of comradeship are only two aspects of this bond. The professional in any walk of life gains success only by paying full attention to the humanities of his organisation. This is vital to produce first-class soldiers ready and willing to go on serving their comrades and their regiment, to the end.

32. Privates Reginald and Bernard Tully. As with others, the evacuated sick or wounded wished to return to their own battalions. It dominated their thoughts when alternative postings might have avoided further danger and hardship.

An example of this bonding within B Company became clear in the behaviour of the brothers Reginald and Bernard Tully. Trained in India, joining the regiment to cross the border into Burma, Bernard Tully, having experienced the early training stages and the arduous weeks of road making west of the Chindwin river, fell sick to tropical disease and was evacuated. Some three weeks later he was fit enough to rejoin, and insisted on returning to his own unit, south of Madaya where within two weeks, his illness, sadly, again caused his evacuation.

Reginald Tully rejoined after a similar hospitalisation at a later date. Often in the thick of our actions, he helped to kill a number of the enemy when his section had captured a bullock cart with a field gun on board, just north of Mandalay, to celebrate his birthday, 4 March. Again, fighting around a clock tower, in the southern suburbs of the city, Tully was under close fire in the skirmish, which not only involved battles with tanks, but also caused the death of Sergeant Heywood, who was hit by a shell splinter that ricocheted off a tank's side. Much later, en route to the south at Meiktila, Reginald Tully succumbed not only to

33. Lance Corporal W.J. Lowe, B Company clerk, May 1945.

34. VJ Day, 1995. The Victory Parade along The Mall, London. Infantry veterans march past HM The Queen. The author, John Hill (nearest the camera), is leading the Royal Berkshire veterans.

malaria, jaundice and round worm disease, but also had previously suffered from appendicitis. Evacuated to India, he was able to request his return to Zeyawadi after recovery to play his part again before the end of the war. Each brother had made special efforts to return to his own unit. High morale had prevailed. B Company was glad to see them back, bruised and battered, yet unbeaten.

CHAPTER 12

Burma (Myanmar) Revisited

Great national events are traditionally commemorated by ceremonial parades on their anniversaries. So it was in 1995, fifty years after the Far East War ended with victory over Japan, when there were great victory celebrations in London, including marches down The Mall. The salute was taken by HM The Queen, accompanied by HRH Prince Philip. The Burma Star contingent included old comrades from those who took part in the campaign, from both the British and Indian Armies. I had the honour to command representatives of our regiment on a summer's day when the heat was almost like that experienced in the Far East. Across the country in cathedrals, churches and at numerous war memorials, it was a time to remember, not only the hard-won victory, but also to pay our respects to all those who had sacrificed their lives for 'King and Country'. There were senior officers marching alongside naval ratings, private soldiers and airmen. There were Gurkhas and Indians alongside their British and Commonwealth counterparts. Nurses and WAS(B)s* completed the contingent. We saw Prince Philip step down from the saluting dais for a short time to join the naval contingent as they marched past HM The Queen. It was 'all for one and one for all', as it had been in 1945.

As part of the commemorative process, both the BBC and ITV gave full coverage, not only of the ceremonial commemorations, but they also created their own historical programmes, showing wartime films of the campaign in Burma. They also helped bring viewers up-to-date

---

* WAS(B) – Women's Auxiliary Services (Burma).

by returning to Burma with a number of the original participants for a visit to some of the battle sites.

Covering the whole campaign, from 1942 to 1945, the BBC chose two other veterans, and me, to accompany them. How lucky we three were to be able to help record the roles we played and visit the relevant battle areas. What follows is a brief description of that visit.

Put yourself in the shoes, or rather boots of us septuagenarians: Richard Rhodes-James, a retired major in the Gurkha Rifles and cypher officer with the second Chindit operations; Bruce Kinloch, a retired major in the 1st and 3rd Gurkha Rifles; a company commander in the Sittang river battle of 1942 with the 17th Indian Division; and myself, John Hill, one-time B Company commander in the 2nd Battalion, The Royal Berkshire Regiment in the 19th Indian Division, which took part in the operations in 1945, from Imphal to Mandalay and beyond. We were all part of a BBC documentary team, visiting Burma in April 1995.

In the Second World War, Japan sought to dominate all the peoples of the Far East and, in particular, destroy the British Empire. Burma was one stepping stone along this route. We had campaigned in this alien land of vast rivers, jungle-covered mountains and hills interspersed with arid plains. Larger than the whole of the land area of the UK and France combined, Burma was a land of stark contrasts. Rangoon and Mandalay were the only two large cities. Endless small villages were scattered sparsely throughout the hinterland. Mosquitoes, flies and jungle crawlies helped to liven us up as we toiled mightily in the dust and dirt in the hot 100° temperatures. In the monsoon, the heavens opened and for weeks on end the rain teemed down. Mud was everywhere, nothing was dry, but soldiering had to continue, unabated. The disastrous retreat across Burma in 1942 was followed by the first counter-offensive in the Arakan, which lead to the turning point in Japanese fortunes, with the great defensive victories of 1944 at Kohima and Imphal, changing the course of the war in our favour. India was saved. These successes led to the 14th Army's advances in 1944 and 1945 and to the final defeat in the field of the once invincible Japanese military machine.

So there we were, selected to accompany Mark Fielder, the BBC producer, and his able team of six, including the well-known presenter Charles Wheeler, to create a documentary film of our *Forgotten War* for the fiftieth anniversary of VJ Day. The planned itinerary took us to Rangoon in order to record the arrival of the 17th Indian Division and the subsequent crucial battle and retreat at the Sittang Bridge in 1942.

Next, we went to Myitkyina for the later Wingate-inspired Chindit operations, behind the Japanese lines. We then travelled down the railway corridor, through the hills and jungles, typical of the 14th Army's advance to Shwebo. Afterwards, we visited the site of the 19th Indian Division's Kyaukmyaung crossing of the Irrawaddy river in 1945, the breakout from the bridgehead at Singu and the capture of Mandalay. A visit to the largest of the three war cemeteries in Burma, at Taukkyan, north of Rangoon, set the final seal on our reporting activities. Tuppence Stone, the indefatigable assistant producer, and Jamieson Koe, the invaluable Burmese 'fixer', had already spent three weeks planning and travelling along our proposed route, clearing every detail with government officials. By aircraft, train, boat and bus, we were to visit all of the important battle areas, travelling some 1,200 miles at the peak of the hot weather, with the temperature between 103°F and 106°F.

The country is run by the State Law and Order Restoration Council (SLORC), headed by the senior general. To make the title sound less aggressive, this council has been renamed The State Peace and Development Council (SPDC). Tight political control was visible everywhere. We were accompanied by 'minders' and soldiers, and had to have government approval for all our movements. External problems persist on the Thai, Chinese, Bangladeshi and Indian borders. Internally, the Karens, Shans and Arakanese were potential troublemakers for the ruling junta. This was not the most auspicious background for a free-ranging tour of battlefields, when tourists normally do not go beyond Mandalay, Rangoon and Pagan.

Finally, the true Burma was to be revealed. Fifty years ago the countryside took second place to a soldier's awareness of the enemy. Who would notice the wild jungle, mountains, hills, rivers and streams, other than as obstacles to progress? Who had time to examine flora and fauna, except as barriers to be hacked down? Who appreciated the beauty of the pagodas or the quaint village houses, except as potential cover for bunkers and strongpoints? Who met the local population, other than as potential spies to be searched?

A glance at the map, on page 19, shows the route that B Company took in 1945. It also covers areas in which the Chindits and the 17th Indian, and other divisions, operated in the earlier years.

One of our first calls was to the Taukkyan War Cemetery, twenty miles north of Rangoon, where 26,380 men, all Allied, Indian, Gurkha, African and British casualties with no known graves, are commemorated on the colonnades of the central memorial, together with 6,368 graves of men gathered from all over Burma. Films were made of my visit to some of the 105 graves of the 2nd Battalion of the Royal Berkshire Regiment, including some B Company men. These included Company Sergeant Major Staples, killed at Kin-U, Private Ravenscroft, Sergeant Heywood DCM, Sergeant Spicer killed at Mandalay, Private Lea, killed at Kabwet, Company Quartermaster Sergeant Freed and Private Hellyer, both killed by an air drop at a DZ near Kyaukmyaung, and Lance Corporal Dale, missing in a swamp at Madaya. Flying to Myitkyina, in the far north, we visited Richard Rhodes-James' Chindit jungle zones at Mogaung, Namkwin, Hopin and the Blackpool Airstrip area. The BBC hired a train with its own sleeping and dining car for our use for the two-day journey south to Mandalay. Travelling at a maximum speed of 20mph over the old and worn rail, we stopped to film wherever and whenever required. Excited crowds greeted us. Some had not seen white people for thirty years, others, never before. Cameraman Mike Fox and sound recorder Bob Webber got some spectacular footage of the railway corridor jungles at Mogaung and at the Bongyang Gorge en route to the old Japanese HQ at Wuntho, where the road from India across the Chindwin river, via Pinlebu, meets the railway. Some twenty trains a day use this railway between Rangoon and the north, and at most halts we were surrounded by crowds of happy smiling faces. From a booklet issued to us in 1944 called *Rubbing Along in Burmese*, and with the help of Jamieson Koe, I managed in Burmese to say 'mingala-ba' (hello), 'ta-ta' (goodbye) and the magical words for 'thank you', 'kyay-zu-tin-bar-de'. The effect on onlookers, especially children, was electrifying! Their eyes opened wider, smiles became broader as the words were repeated back to me, again and again.

Why are the Burmese apparently such happy people? They live in a Communist state, discouraged from independent, political thought, living in a third-world economy, where only government officials and favoured people have any real wealth. When cowed, they show some respect for authority and a fear of political unrest. Human rights violations persist. However, to the short-term visitor, there is little noticeable misery or squalor, as most places are clean, religious observance is everywhere and the population is at work. It is an enigma to western eyes to see and meet so many smiling, co-operative and cheerful people everywhere. Almost with regret, we left our friendly guard and the Burmese version of the Orient Express at Shwebo, and transferred

35. *Mandalay Hill from the walls and moat of Fort Dufferin, 1995.*

36. *Taukkyan cemetery, north of Rangoon, 1995.*

to two minibuses, bumping and jolting eighty miles to Mandalay, via the 19th Indian Division's 1945 Irrawaddy crossing, at Kyaukmyaung. Here, the enemy had deployed a large concentration of artillery to prevent our breakout. After bitter fighting at Pear Hill and Minban Taung, the Japanese were defeated and the road to Mandalay was opened.

Seated in a country boat, walking across rickety bridges or driving at a maximum speed of 15mph, Charles Wheeler portrayed our progress for the camera. We wondered if these roads had ever been remetalled since the days of British colonial rule.

At Mandalay Hill, up and down the steps of this holy site, with its host of gleaming gold-topped pagodas, we recorded some wartime highlights, such as setting the enemy alight with petrol in a tunnel, and blowing in the roof of a last-ditch position. Next, we went into the city for street scenes and a visit to St Mary's Roman Catholic church, where a Japanese medical officer was taken prisoner while praying at the altar. Sister Mary Andrew, now in charge, offered prayers for us all.

We returned to Rangoon to film Bruce Kinloch in the docks, where he had landed with 600 mules and horses for the Gurkha Brigade. Then we went on to the Sittang river bridge, eighty miles to the east. Here, in 1942, half of our defending force was left on the east bank, where the bridge was controversially blown up to prevent the Japanese from reaching Rangoon. The local Burmese military commanders were particularly concerned about our presence with cameras in this sensitive area, close to the Thai border.

Space does not allow a full description of the unique religious water festival, celebrating the Burmese New Year (held at the same time as Easter). Suffice to say, the whole population takes to the streets for a minimum of three days. Everyone drenches everyone else with water from every receptacle available, including fire hoses! Under this sometimes unwanted barrage do smiles subside? They do not! The message is, 'have fun and enjoy the experience if you can, but always smile!'

So ended a breathtaking return to a remarkable country. It was a once-in-a-lifetime opportunity to revisit our old battlegrounds and pay tribute to all those who died fighting for freedom and democracy against an inhumane, cruel and repressive foe. It was a chance to take a glimpse of a culture very different from our own, in a land unspoilt by modern buildings and where the natural state still dominates the environment.

In making this historic documentary of the *Forgotten Army*, the BBC and its producer Mark Fielder deserve the greatest credit for the

37. St Mary's Roman Catholic Church, Mandalay, with Sister Mary Andrew, 1995.

38. The author searching for graves in the British War Cemetery, Rangoon, 1995.

sheer professionalism, enthusiasm and dedication of the whole team. Former members of the Indian Army might say, 'shabash BBC' ('thank you BBC'). I end with the more colloquial Burmese, 'kyay-zu-tin-bar-de BBC' (also 'thank you BBC').

Above all, this was a dramatic reminder to each of us of the sacrifices of so many British, Indian and Commonwealth and Allied servicemen in the defence of Britain and her Empire and the free world, and also how Burma and other countries had been freed from the Japanese when peace was declared. The rebuilding of the country's economy was another major achievement. As the years have moved on, the government's rigid political control has shown its true colours. The human cost to the Burman, and his cheerful acceptance of the hand of fate, has cast a slur on the political military machine, which keeps the masses in poverty while enriching the ruling military caste.

This realisation left us with the sad reflection that all efforts to remove the Japanese and create opportunity for an equitable democratic society had been seriously tarnished by the policies of the present rulers of Burma, now renamed Myanmar.

Summary and Conclusion

The first ten chapters of this work have described examples of the experiences of soldiers serving their 'King and Country', both in training for war and in action in the 14th Army in India and Burma, in 1944 and 1945 with the 19th Indian (Dagger) Division. The eleventh chapter has attempted to fill in the psychological backdrop to all our activities, in order to highlight the spiritual dimension ever present and mention topics not usually considered, but of great relevance when times were tough and difficult. Together, the chapters illustrate the problems faced and overcome in an infantry unit by those who served in its ranks, whether as junior leaders or as private soldiers. They offer an insight into the need for continuous detailed training and obedience to orders, whatever the circumstances. They show what the term 'duty' to the regiment, and to their comrades, really means 'when the chips are down' in the long, drawn-out uncertainties and confusion of war, as it was experienced in the concluding months of the Burma Campaign.

My earlier book *China Dragons* set out the general framework and collective engagements and activities in which B Company, 2nd Battalion of the Royal Berkshire Regiment was involved as part of the 19th Indian (Dagger) Division. This later account has filled in a number of events describing incidents and life at a more down-to-earth soldier level during our many operations.

The nature of war on the Burma front was markedly different from most other theatres, especially when volumes of firepower are compared. In Europe, and in the desert campaigns in Africa against the Germans and Italians, the availability of aircraft, ships and guns resulted in heavy bombardments and mass assaults supported by tanks and other tracked vehicles. Both in attack and defence operations were often carried out, and directly controlled at brigade and divisional levels. The supply of ammunition, flame throwers and mines in Europe and Africa was on a huge scale, but impossible to match in the administrative nightmare created by the climate, terrain and primitive communications in Burma. In Europe it was unusual for soldiers to find themselves in direct close combat for long periods – even in the Italian Campaign, where the terrain created similar conditions. Relief from shot and shell routinely occurred in other theatres, while reserve formations and units took over. Shortage of men and the wide divisional fronts, necessitated by the 14th Army's deployment, meant that soldiers in the forward units in Burma experienced maximum exposure to enemy infantry weapons and to their close support gunfire. Surprise by ambush was a continuous threat. Thus, the norm was close-quarter skirmishing, day in and day out for most infantry units, with gunner and tank support from time to time as a bonus. Relief from operations was seldom possible. The classic infantryman's battle drill: down, crawl, observe and fire, was put to full use as the war progressed through Burma.

Most importantly, these stories demonstrate how all the facets which make a trained soldier – knowledge, discipline, endurance, comradeship and regimental spirit – come together to create high morale. Without such morale, normal infantry soldiers would bend and crack under stress. But with it nothing will stop him overcoming the fear, uncertainty, turmoil and danger of the battlefield to defeat his enemy. Morale is the vital ingredient for a soldier, particularly, as in these stories, when faced with the worst of natural hazards in the tropics and a tough suicidal enemy against him. Perversely, perhaps, the best indication of a true soldier's worth is that, as in Burma, men go on and on, serving their regiment, sub-unit and mates to the best of their abilities, whatever the difficulties and conditions in which they find themselves, training and acclimatisation being essential aids to success.

I have described ten separate incidents. There were, however, many similar actions and skirmishes with the enemy during some six months of aggressive campaigning by this 'spearhead' unit of the 14th Army. Involved during this period was a grand total of some 196 of all ranks who came under my command. Of this number, thirty-nine were killed and an additional 112 became battle casualties. These severe losses are summarised in Appendix 2, Annex E.

Service and dedication, battle skills and endurance, cheerful comradeship and self denial, aided by regimental and unit *esprits de corps*, built our high morale. For some, a spiritual or religious dimension gave us belief in ourselves and in our cause. It was almost incidental that some officers, NCOs and men of B Company did receive two Military Crosses, one Distinguished Conduct Medal, four Military Medals and two Mentioned in Dispatches, when so many actions by the majority of soldiers, as illustrated in this account, remained 'all in a day's or night's work', with no medals awarded, nor expected. 'So what?' they would say. 'We were there. We did our best and we were lucky to survive.'

Over the centuries the infantry of the line have always borne the brunt of the numerous campaigns that have marked the progress of humanity towards its destiny. Empires have come and gone, nations have expanded and contracted as political will and military power have ebbed and flowed around the globe. Governments, in the last resort, and even at present, have had to rely on military forces to defend their principles or territory.

As modern technology has developed, so co-operation and contact between nations have transformed the political scene. It could be argued that the demise of the last great empire, The British Empire, and the independence given to millions of hitherto subordinate peoples, coupled with lessons learnt from the waging of two world wars and numerous lesser military settlements, would lead to a pacific approach in future political problems. It would be a great comfort if the twenty-first century saw an end to military force to solve intractable disputes between nations. As the twentieth century drew to its close, the world still resounded to the clash of military armaments, even between countries that had signed up to the principles of international law embodied in the United Nations Charter. So how much realistic hope is there that defence forces, in general, and the infantry of the line, in particular, will have any part to play in the years ahead?

Today, any nation which, unilaterally, cancelled its entire budget for defence forces would be foolhardy in the extreme. Collectively, even the United Nations is light years short of such an optimistic stance. So wars, of various scales, seem likely to continue demanding the presence of defence forces. The threat from nuclear fission and weapons of mass destruction at one end of the scale, and the need for armed soldiers as internal security policemen at the other end, indicate the necessity for employment of highly trained and fully supported infantry for the foreseeable future.

The lessons of the past offer the men who serve in the new regiments of infantry a brief glimpse of their recent forebears at the front-line level, carrying forward the old traditions of the regiment. Particularly at this time, the Royal Gloucestershire, Berkshire and Wiltshire Regiment (RGBW), with its regular and territorial battalion, may gain some knowledge and pride from what is written here about the men who served in B Company, 2nd Battalion Royal Berkshire Regiment and whom they have succeeded in today's Army.

Those who served in B Company or who were in close support, and at the time of writing were still around over fifty years after the events described, include B Company's Corporal (later Company Sergeant Major) Ron Sibley MM of Poole, Private Ken Wells of Littlehampton, Lance Corporal Bill Lowe of Coventry, Privates Reg and Bernard Tully of Ferndown, Private (later Company Sergeant Major) Theo Shave of Sherborne and Sergeant Bertie King of Christchurch who was in administration. The muleteers include Private Wilf Bagwell of Blandford Forum and Private Harry Sanders of Nottingham. Corporal T. Pearce of Reading was the signaller, while Corporal Terry Ashby of Halstead was in the Pioneer Platoon. The Intelligence Section included Corporal Arthur Pike of Tiverton and Private Gilbert Scott Selwyn of Wolverhampton.

The lucky survivors will all remember their journeys home to England – flying out by the twin-engined Dakota aircraft from forward airfields, to land in India near Chittagong or Calcutta, then across the continent by train to Deolali transit camp before joining a troopship for the final leg of the journey, via the Suez Canal or the Cape. The whole procedure took six weeks or more before docking in Liverpool. Others made the whole journey by ship from Rangoon, via Columbo in Sri Lanka and Cape Town or Suez.

Demob suits were issued to all before returning to civilian life in their home towns after a final visit to the regimental depot at Reading. For some of those posted to the Far East, up to four years had elapsed before they could be reunited with their families. In today's world such a period of overseas service, away from home and family in the UK, without a break would not be acceptable. At the end of the war, not only was the system accepted as part of wartime service, but the comradeship it engendered within the regiment was enhanced, and among those wartime mates it endures to this day.

40. War graves near Tamokso, forty miles south of Mandalay . . .

42. . . . and south of Mandalay Hill. All the wooden crosses were made by the Pioneer Platoon under the guidance of Corporal Terry Ashby.

41. The end of the day – Company Sergeant Major R.H. Staples was killed in action at Kin-U and is interred at Taukkyan Cemetery, Rangoon.
.

42. Wreaths are laid at the cenotaph, Brock Barracks, Reading, every year on 11 November at the regimental cenotaph in commemoration of the regiment's war dead.

43. The author, John Hill, wearing his medals.

The popular song *Take me back to dear old Blighty,** often suitably expressed in soldier language, showed the feelings and cheerful humour of soldiers resigned to service in out-of-the-way places, while waiting their turn for repatriation after a dose of 'Doolalli Tap'** or a touch of the 'Doolallies', as it was popularly know by those at home.

Nostalgic recollections of the lighter side of soldiering out east are balanced by memories of those comrades who did not return and whose remains lie in the Commonwealth War Cemeteries in Burma, or are commemorated on the war memorials at Taukkyan and elsewhere. The epitaphs at the end of this book pay their own tribute to so many who served their country honourably and who paid the ultimate price in 1944 and 1945.

As described in chapter twelve, to commemorate the fiftieth anniversary of the end of the war I returned to Burma where I was lucky

---

* 'Blighty' – a soldier's name for home coined from the Hindu word 'bilarti' meaning 'far away'

** 'Doolalli Tap' – anyone with service out East was stigmatised particularly by those at home with certain madness on passing through the Deolali Transit Camp at Bombay after years of heat and tropical hazards.

enough to visit many wartime battle areas, to relive the past and help bring them to life through the BBC and ITV programmes. The programmes themselves were fitting tributes to all our soldiers in their long hard service in the inhospitable terrain, where the men of B Company, and their supporting arms, finally defeated the enemy.

As with the importance of the perfect state of nirvana to the Buddhist in his strivings for the next world, let us remember our Christian message of hope and reconciliation for all those who did their duty in Burma.

Infantry soldiers will always be needed, as they have been through the centuries, to maintain our defence capabilities and play their part in overseas deployments, as national foreign policy may demand. Perhaps these experiences of 'Slim's Burma Boys' may help them to be prepared for future conflict, if all peaceful means fail to prevent armed struggles between nations.

APPENDIX 1

Annex A: Burma, the Country and its People

Landscape

'For the wind is in the palm trees and the temple bells they say,
Come you back you British soldier, come you back to Mandalay.'
Rudyard Kipling – 'Mandalay'

The two sketch maps on page 19 show the position of Burma in South-East Asia and the relevant outline locations of the cities, towns, rivers and hills. Burma covers a land area of some 261,000sq m – three times the size of the UK. The Bay of Bengal and the Andaman Sea lie to the south and south-west. Bangladesh and India are located to the west. Thailand and Laos are to the east and south-east, and to the north lies China and Tibet.

Within its borders, the Kachin Hills cover the north. In the west, the Arakan Hills and Chin Hills run toward Bangladesh. To the east of the central plains, the Shan plateau dominates. To the south, the long narrow strip of Tenasserim runs down the side of the Andaman Sea to Thailand, towards Malaysia. Burma is some 1,200 miles long, from north to south, and 620 miles wide across its centre. The mighty Irrawaddy river rises in the Himalayas, flowing down the centre of the country until dispersing in a wide delta into the Andaman Sea, a distance of 1,680 miles. Its width, some 450 miles from its mouth, is often not less than 1,200 yards. The fast flowing Chindwin, Sittang, Salween and Shweli rivers also descend from north to south and help to split the terrain, with benefits to trade and agriculture. Along their banks, and up into the mountains and hills, stretch verdant pastures, endless scrub, bamboo and massive teak forests. To the west, the Kaladan river

133

flows past the borders with Bangladesh and splits the mountain areas for some 200 miles to the Bay of Bengal.

Campaigning in such a land, where marshes and streams also impeded movement, posed major problems for military command-ers. Where these natural hazards for soldiers in combat are added to the tropical heat and humidity, it will be realised that all the supply services, in both armies, had unique circumstances to overcome, the lines of communication and supply stretching back for a thousand miles and more. Tanks and other tracked vehicles were often unable to support infantry operations. Gunner support and close-air support were, however, available for many of our major assaults, and resup-ply was often by air. Burma was an infantryman's war in every way. Foot soldiers were essential for overcoming both the environment and the enemy.

Climate

The Tropic of Cancer lies across the country, thus the temperature varies from an average 80° to 90°F from November to February, fol-lowed by hot weather from March to May of about 112°F. The skies at night are clear, so that navigation by the stars, which we had trained for, became possible. Sirius and Cassiopeia were visible but not the North Star. The monsoon rains descend in tempestuous downpours from June to October, bringing the temperature down to 60°F, at its lowest. Humidity is high with energy-sapping results for soldiers engaged in long marches and aggressive action. In the hills and mountains, the temperate climate above 1,000 feet from the central plains brought relief, making life more bearable. The move-ment of vehicles and tanks became almost impossible during the monsoon period, but between October and May ground operations were correspondingly helped by the dry weather on the plains. The need then for a steady supply of water to prevent dehydration was a major concern, with water sterilisation kits a life-saving necessity. The vagaries of the heat and wet conditions produced a wide vari-ety of wild animals and birds. Some of our oral signals used in the jungles between sub-units, in the absence of radio communication, attempted to imitate animal calls to confuse the enemy. Insects and reptiles were encountered everywhere.Bites from crawling insects, ticks, mosquitoes and other flies caused typhus, malaria or dengue fever. The need for medical injections and care were vital to maintain our battle fitness. Deer roamed free in many areas, and their noises were often mistaken for the enemy.

Population

Some 45 million people live in Burma, of which 75 per cent live on the central plains, mostly in the rural areas. But also significant numbers live in the large cities and towns, such as in the capital Rangoon, Mandalay, Prome, Pegu and Moulmein. Originally, the country was infiltrated by Chinese and Tibetans from the north where the centre of Burma was divided up into groups of Burmans. Around the central plain in the hills and mountain areas, ethnic Burmese were surrounded by the similarly ethnic tribes of Kachin, Rakhine, Chin, Mon, Karen, Wa and Shan. Proud of their separate origins and identity, conflicts have been waged by them with those Burmese in the centre, through the ages. To this day, an on-going guerrilla war continues to give the current military government much concern, bringing harsh retaliation on dissidents. During the British occupation, and especially during the Second World War, the Karen, Kachin, Shans and others allied themselves closely to our forces, against the Japanese, later to counter the Burmese government's plans for integration and dictatorship.

In 1944 and 1945 most of the population left their towns and villages to take refuge in the countryside, until military operations finished. Very few Burmese were encountered during the many months of campaigning.

Economy

Burma's economy is essentially based on agriculture – mainly cereals, rice and fishing. The majority of the population live in rural areas, working on the land and waterways. Although rubies from Mogok and minerals from the hill areas produce high revenue from exports, the growing and export of opium, originally for medical use in the hospitals of the Empire, provides steady sales to drug barons. Perhaps the trade in teak remains the most stable and important asset.

Teak trees are felled, drawn by herds of elephants to the rivers and floated down to the depots and mills for processing and loading onto ships. Likewise, the ubiquitous bamboo, growing profusely through-out the country, is tied onto rafts and sent for local and international use. During the Second World War the availability of local boats and rafts enabled speedier movement over the terrain. River crossings were made easier by the ad hoc assembly of local craft to augment military assault boats, which were often unavailable.

Religion

A British soldier, whatever his religion or belief, is made fully aware of the need to respect the religious observances and icons of any country through which he campaigns. Burma was no exception. In Burma, since the sixth century BC, Buddhism, deriving its source from Hinduism, came to be the guiding religious philosophy for all the inhabitants of the country. The Buddha, to whom Burmans pay respect and tribute for his teachings, is enshrined in pagodas and temples throughout the land. In all main cities and towns, the Buddha is worshipped. The Shwedagon pagoda, in Rangoon, is probably the finest in the land. The upkeep of all religious buildings is met by charitable donations. No expense appears to have been spared. The Buddhist is taught to maintain eight principles to grant enlightenment and reach perfection in this life. The eight principles which will also achieve peace and tranquillity in the next life are good speech, views, intentions, actions, livelihood, effort, good thoughts and contemplations. Within these principles there can be no murder, theft, lust, lying or alcohol.

To those of us young soldiers, little, if anything, was known of these laudable aims while we moved through the country – only seldom seeking, and even more seldom, meeting any local people. The inhabitants of today cannot find it easy to keep to these principles. One of these, no alcohol, was certainly not followed in April 1995 when I returned to the country and attended their Water Festival. The largest exhibit was sponsored by a local brewery, and their beer was readily available. The young are encouraged to serve in their monasteries and temples as noviciates for some few years, as part of their service to others. While under the control of monks, they are supported by local charities and dressed in simple smocks. Small groups with their bowls for food and offerings are seen everywhere today.

Politics

The early history of Burma shows how the central plains astride the Irrawaddy river influenced many local empires which have come and gone. The Burmese were the subject and victim of many incursions

44. *Teak trees being rafted down the Irrawady.*

45. *One of the 3,000 elephants in Burma, logging across a chaung.*

and uprisings over the borders to the north, long before British rule was established following the Burma Wars between 1824 and 1886. From this point, the British ruled the country, opening it up to international trade, especially in teak, minerals and opium.

During the 1920s nationalist movements in Burma began to resist British rule. During the Second World War, the Japanese were seen as a vehicle to help remove the British, and so Burmese Nationalists began to work for independence.

By 1945 the Japanese, who many Burmese had supported, were in retreat. The Burmese, in a tactical change, backed the British, until the Japanese surrender, when the Nationalists again began to resist British rule, thus continuing the movement which, some three years later, led to independence under Aung San and his successors.

The communist/socialist elements now took over, assassinating Aung San and his cabinet to establish a police state. Since then, this dictatorship has controlled all activities, and after free elections in 1990, it refused to accept the popular vote for a new democratic government. Aung San's daughter, Daw Aung San Suu Kyi, who led the movement, was placed under house arrest. The existing rulers, The State Peace and Development Council, led by Army generals, continue to dominate all political thought and activity. Freedom of thought is no longer permitted for the population. The tribes on the boundaries still continue to resist, but so far to no avail, while the rest of the world looks on.

Annex B: Translation of a Leaflet Dropped by Air to the Japanese in March 1945

Meiktila (Burma) has been occupied by our Joint Force. Taji has also been occupied by our strong new English attached force. All Japanese soldiers! What is this all about?

Although you have been fighting bravely in this war, you have no chance to win; our strong English mechanized and armoured force crossed the Irrawaddy river and have entered the plain area and are forging eastwards in a mopping up operation which is only developing.

Isn't it so that Meiktila and Taji have already been occupied by our Army? During this attack your garrison forces have been annihilated and our successful strong attacking force is turning towards Mandalay.

46. B Company triumph at Kin-u, 1945.

How do you feel about losing these two important cities? If you look at the map on the reverse of this paper you will see clearly how the Japanese Army is menaced by our great manoeuvre.

Then, why has this situation developed? The reason is your life line (supply line) has been cut by our Army – To put it concretely: rein-forcement of your force is impossible. Re-supply cannot be effected. You cannot receive medicine for your sick and wounded. You can't re-supply yourselves with ammunition. And above this, your present pitiful condition has been brought on by your blundering command-er's incompetancy.

Your incompetent commander is the one who has led you into your miserable condition. He is the guilty one. Thus, while you are cornered, our English Army is charging from the north of Mandalay, to the east of the Irrawaddy river and are in Mandalay's suburbs.

Knowing you have no hope, why are you continuing to fight? Death and starvation are the only things awaiting you. I wonder what will be awaiting you? I wonder what will be the gain in the sacrifice of your life?

We are full of admiration for you. There is no reason for you to continue this useless fight. We welcome you to come over to our side. We give a solemn promise that we will treat you well. After the war, in order to promote peace and prosperity within your nation, and to establish a New Japan, we need your co-operation DECIDE QUICKLY! IT IS NOT TOO LATE!

APPENDIX 2

Annex A: A Brief History of the Regiment

Slim's Burma Boys is dedicated to the steadfastness and bravery of the NCOs and men of B Company, a particular sub-unit of the 2nd Battalion Royal Berkshire Regiment. It is thanks to material provided by some of the survivors that their stories and connected comments can be written down as an important addition to those contained in *China Dragons*, which covered B Company's training for war and, later on, actions in Burma from a general and overall perspective of the campaign. Both in training and in war, the company served alongside Punjabi Muslims from the 8/12th Frontier Force Regiment, Gurkhas from Nepal in the 4/4th Gurkha Rifles and Sikhs from north-west India in the 11th Sikh Regiment. This was a typical mixture of many races, creeds and religions who worked happily together as comrades. The activities of B Company thus play an honourable part in the long and distinguished history of its successors in the modern Army, the Royal Gloucestershire, Berkshire and Wiltshire Regiment. To understand the traditions that motivate and encourage soldiers of the infantry, this short note provides an outline.

The service of the regiment starts with the formation of the first of its forebears, the 28th Foot in 1694, and continues down the years with the founding of the 49th, 61st, 62nd, and 55th Regiments of Foot. All were known by their numbers in seniority. In 1782 they acquired links to particular counties. In 1881, the Cardwell Reforms reorganised these regiments into the Gloucestershire Regiment, the Berkshire Regiment (created Royal in 1885) and the Wiltshire Regiment, to which was added the 99th of Foot. Each regiment maintained two regular battalions and incorporated the local rifle volunteers as TA battalions. Militia battalions were continued for reinforcements, as well as a training depot within the regimental district.

After the end of the Second World War, each regiment was reduced to one regular battalion. Some eleven years later, an additional reorganisation was ordered – in 1959 the Royal Berkshire and Wiltshire Regiments amalgamated to form the Duke of Edinburgh's Royal Regiment, with the Gloucestershire Regiment being left intact. In 1994, with continuing reductions in the infantry, the Gloucestershire Regiment joined the Duke of Edinburgh's Royal Regiment to form the new Royal Gloucestershire, Berkshire and Wiltshire Regiment, absorbing the volunteer territorial battalions of the Wessex Regiment. The future of this fine regiment, after much discussion, has been decided. It has been transferred into the Light Division, and has merged with the Devon and Dorset Regiment to become, by virtue of seniority, 1st Battalion, The Rifles, enjoying the luxury of a permanent base, Chepstow, and a new and challenging role of Commando Battalion.

A short but comprehensive description of most of the events which form the history of the regiment is available under the title *Our Laurels are Green*[*] from the Regimental Headquarters in Gloucester and Salisbury. It describes the many countries in which the regiment has served since its original formation. Published in 1997, the events in Burma in 1944 and 1945 are briefly chronicled, but detailed descriptions of all the battles and engagements by all the regiments could not be included.

Between 1942 and 1945, five battalions of the regiment served in Burma, including the 1st and 10th Battalions of the Gloucestershire Regiment, the 1st and 2nd Battalions of the Royal Berkshire Regiment and the 1st Battalion of the Wiltshire Regiment. Each battalion has its own story to tell of experiences fighting the Japanese in the tropical heat and monsoons of the jungles, mountains and plains. The most crucial accounts come from the 1st Battalion Royal Berkshire Regiment, which played such a prominent part in the defence of India at the battle of Kohima on its North-East Frontier.

This battle is acknowledged by most historians to have been the turning point in the war against Japan in the Far East. Kohima and its aftermath led directly to the defeat of the Japanese in Burma and to their biggest defeat anywhere on land. In this defeat, the 2nd Battalion

[*] Robin Grist, *Our Laurels are Green*, Forces and Corporate Publishing Ltd, 1997.

Royal Berkshire Regiment played a full part. These chapters have provided a selection of examples of the dedication and service in just one company of one infantry battalion at war, replicating similar regimental service around the world throughout the previous 300 years of its existence. Down-to-earth, solid achievements, which overcame all difficulties of terrain and climate, illustrate the part played by the NCOs and men of B Company, 2nd Battalion Royal Berkshire Regiment in defeating the Japanese and in so doing, helped to bring the Second World War to an end.

Annex B: Order of the Day

By Lieutenant General Sir William Slim KCB, CBE, DSO, MC, General Officer Commander-in-Chief Fourteenth Army

You have won the battle for central Burma. It has been no easy triumph. You have won it against the obstacles of nature, and against numerous, well-equipped and vicious enemy. You have earned victory by the skill, boldness and resolution of corps, divisional and brigade commanders, and by your refusal to let difficulties overcome you, by your grim endurance, unquenchable fighting spirit and magnificent audacity.

You have advanced for hundreds of miles at unexampled speed over mountains, through jungles and across arid plains, making your own roads, cutting your own tracks, building your own boats, and always against cunning, fanatical opposition. You have forced the heavily defended crossings of two great rivers. These crossings you carried out with meagre equipment, supplemented only by what you could make with your own hands or capture from the enemy. You have driven seven enemy divisions from long prepared positions of his own choosing, which he was ordered to hold to the last. He has fled leaving 18,000 counted corpses on the ground and over 300 guns in your hands.

Every corps, division and brigade has played its part in this Fourteenth Army victory. None could have done what it did without the help of the others. There could not have been any victory without the constant, ungrudging support of the Allied Air Forces. The skill, endurance and gallantry of our comrades in the air, on which we have learnt so confidently to rely, have never failed us. It is their victory as much as ours.

Every man of the Fourteenth Army and of the Air Forces which flew with it can be proud of his share in this battle. I cannot tell you how proud I am of the men I command. That pride is felt too in your homes, in the Britain, India, Nepal and Africa you have defended, and in the Burma you are liberating.

We have advanced far towards final victory in Burma, but we have one more stage before it is achieved. We have heard a lot about the Road to Mandalay: now we are on the Road from Mandalay.

The Japanese are mustering their whole remaining strength in Burma to bar our path. When we meet them again, let us do to them what we have done before, and this time even more thoroughly.

8 April 1945
W.J. Slim Lieutenant General
General Officer Commander-in-Chief

Annex C: Military Organizations, 1944–5

In 1944 and 1945, as part of the 14th Army in Burma, the 2nd Battalion Royal Berkshire Regiment was one of the three infantry battalions in the 98th Brigade of the 19th Indian (Dagger) Division. The other two battalions in the 98th Brigade were the 8/12th Frontier Force Regiment and the 4/4th Gurkha Rifles.

A division totalled some 15,000 of all ranks and included three infantry brigades, each of three battalions, with supporting arms and services. These included divisional armour, a medium machine-gun battalion, an HQ defence battalion and a divisional reconnaissance battalion, four artillery regiments and divisional Royal Engineers, Royal Army service corps, medical, electrical and mechanical engineers and various other smaller supporting units. Without such support, both operational and administrative, our achievements would not have been possible. Also not to be left out were the RAF, who bombed and strafed the enemy, and dropped supplies when the situation on the ground made normal resupply impossible.

A British infantry battalion comprised 800 of all ranks, comprising Battalion HQ (command and control), HQ Company (administration and supply), Support Company (heavy weapons, i.e. mortars, medium machine-guns and anti-tank guns), four rifle companies, each

47. Field Marshal Slim – 'Uncle Bill'.

with three rifle platoons, and each of these with rifle sections, each of eight men.

The nominal, full strength of a rifle company was 112, but more often than not it stood at only seventy of all ranks, due to sickness and casualties. For transport, we boasted a Jeep with its trailer and four mules.

Annex D: Training for Jungle Warfare

When, in December 1941, a substantial force of Japanese troops crossed the Sino-Burmese border near Lashio, the British Empire in South-East Asia faced a new threat of huge and unknown dimensions. Not only were the Japanese veterans of several years' fighting, but they were well prepared, lightly loaded and enjoyed the element of surprise. In contrast, empire forces in the main consisted of one poorly trained, locally recruited 1st Burma Division. In India, the Army was fully committed to internal security, or in other words 'aid to the civil power'. Little or no time, nor resources, had been allotted to training for jungle warfare.

Soon, a second Japanese thrust northward from the Thai border threatened the British strategy, which had been to reinforce hastily with untrained units from India, holding on to Rangoon at all costs. Despite the arrival of the 17th Indian Division, platoons and companies, hastily withdrawing, were frequently ambushed from jungle positions by the tenacious and experienced enemy. The retreat became a rout.

Long-standing concepts of tactical movement, both by individuals, as well as collectively, were to be challenged and changed forever. At last, new and improved infantry weapons and better, more accurate artillery for close support began to arrive, as well as field radios and even small numbers of American-built tanks. However, even the limited Arakan offensive in December 1942, while providing very useful experience and boosting morale, achieved only local success.

There was a clear need to revolutionise training for jungle warfare. This started in 1943 with the formation of South-East Asia command, and with it higher priority for availability of new weapons and aircraft. A key to the future success was the formation of divisional battle schools. One of the best of these was that of 19th Indian Division at Chingleput, in southern India. It was one of the best known for simulating battle conditions. Those who attended these schools had the most realistic battle scenarios imposed upon them. Individuals practising fieldcraft, fire and movement under a hail of shots fired as close to them as safely possible, were taught to keep their nerve and continue with the pressures of the simulated battle situation and to pass their knowledge on to their units. Most men experienced their first realistic shelling by artillery at these schools. So, each man was taught continuously how to maintain and use his weapon by endless live firing, to shoot accurately while under simulated fire by shot and shell, to run, crawl and assault fortifications, dig trenches, and lay barbed wire. He was also taught to patrol through all types of terrain and lay ambushes, learn the vital importance of camouflage, find his way across country by compass bearings and the stars, learn map reading with all its complexities and operate by day and by night – especially by night for long periods.

Individual training also needed day-to-day discipline with water, food, rest, clothing, cleanliness, latrines, medical supplies and especially silence in the jungle.

Collective training could only be of real value when all these individual training techniques had been fully mastered. Movement by individuals, sections and platoons through the jungles, over hills, shrub and plains, across streams and rivers, as well as modifying tactical formations without losing control while moving, halting, attacking or defending in each new location, was vital.

APPENDIX 2

48. *The Ava Bridge at Mandalay.*

Practising evacuation of casualties, with and without stretchers, communication between and within groups, either verbally or by signs, and endlessly learning how the enemy would be likely to act or react as operations developed was equally important.

In practical terms, three of the most difficult individual problems to instil were firstly, the need for silence in the jungle and the learning of special sounds to replace word of mouth; secondly, the forbidding of smoking* during jungle movement when a unit's concealment could be gratuitously jeopardised by the smoke and smell, with dire results; thirdly, quiet but careful assessment by each individual soldier, especially the section commanders, of signs of Japanese movements, and the fire and movement needed to neutralise and kill the enemy. The Japanese often gave their presence away by careless smoke from their fires. They also gave off a strange body smell which helped British patrols to be aware of the enemy before contact was established in the jungle. Finally, there was the need to counter fear by well-planned, positive and aggressive action without incurring unnecessary casualties.

Superimposed on individual training and collective training, the detailed knowledge of co-operation with tanks created their own dis-

---

* Smoking of cigarettes was universally accepted as a morale raiser in all armies in the Second World War. Few men did not puff cigarettes or smoke pipes.

147

49. B Company mules led by muleteers Privates Buckle and Bagwell.

ciplines, in both obtaining and giving close support in attack and defence at the individual soldier's level. Practical training for war in Burma took into account all these extra skills. The results were plain for all to see during the long weeks of practice exercises against simulated enemy forces. British, Gurkha, Indian and African, each took turns to imitate Japanese action and operations, being 'attacked', posing as the enemy. Confidence was gained through battle drills; overcoming hostile terrain in the jungles, across hills, through swamps and over trackless scrub desert; 'know-how' was learnt and relearnt both before combat was joined, and in any sparse gaps during breaks in the fighting itself after moving over the frontier into Burma.

'Tom, Dick and Harry' became true warriors. Their morale was at a very high level, nurtured and encouraged by the successful operational plans made at the highest level within which we all operated.

In the 14th Army, we were all truly 'Slim's Burma Boys'. The first few engagements demonstrated to all that we were more than a match for our opponents in this unique climate and terrain. The GOC 19th

Indian Division Major General T.W. Rees referred particularly to our Royal Berkshire Regiment battalion when he was interviewed by the BBC in March 1945 in the northern outskirts of Mandalay. 'The men are very dusty, they've been going all out – more than all out. I've never, never seen such enthusiasm. It is this undoubtedly that is keeping them going. They feel the prize [of defeating the enemy] is worth the effort.'

The men of B Company, 2nd Battalion Royal Berkshire Regiment did their duty to the nation in India and Burma in 1944 and 1945, as had so many of their regimental predecessors in many historic wars fought in foreign lands. As their company commander, I was in a unique position to live, and to see and learn, at first hand, how the maintenance of morale in all circumstances was paramount to success. On a lower descriptive level, I was able to see and understand what made men tick when times were at their worst, especially in the face of the enemy. These short accounts therefore illuminate the tasks of all infantrymen who served their regiments and each other so loyally in the alien climatic conditions of the Second World War.

The modern generation of soldiers serving the nation in the 'push button' warfare age need have no doubt that the future will be just as

50. B Company en route south near Toungoo.

demanding as the past. The Royal Berkshire Regiment's successor may be sure that international terrorism, intractable international disputes and the need to maintain an acceptable standard of humanity and tolerance around the world, will demand their presence as infantrymen, again and again, to restore peace and goodwill. As in 1944 and 1945, B Company's successors will find no soft options in their soldiers' role.

As a symbol of loyalty to our Queen and Country, and to comrades in arms, the message of hope and faith when times are hard and the going gets rough, endures forever.

Annex E: Awards and Casualties, B Company, 2nd Battalion The Royal Berkshire Regiment

Summary of Battle Casualties, December 1944–June 1945

	Killed/died of wounds/missing	Wounded	TOTAL
OFFICERS	1	4	5
COMPANY SERGEANT MAJOR	1	–	1
COMPANY QUARTERMASTER SERGEANT	1	–	1
SERGEANTS	5	5	10
CORPORALS AND PRIVATES	31	64	95
TOTAL	39	73	112

APPENDIX 2

Summary of Honours and Awards, December 1944–June 1945

OFFICERS	Military Cross	2
	Mentioned in Dispatches	1
SERGEANTS	Distinguished Conduct Medals	1
	Military Medals	1
CORPORALS AND PRIVATES	Military Medals	3
	Mentioned in Dispatches	1
TOTAL		9

Battle Casualties, December 1944–June 1945

30 Killed in Action				
Date	Place	Number	Name	Remarks
26 December	Thityabin	5334026	Sgt Williams	
27 December	North of Leitku	?	Lt J. Ridley	
28 December	North of Leitku	5347880	Pte Pridham	
31 December	Leitku	5348560	Pte Mason	
7 January	Kin-U	6403548	CSM Staples	
8 January	Kin-U	14642948	Pte Horton	
8 January	Kin-U	14565301	Pte Hall	
8 January	Kin-U	14335060	Pte Jones	
8 January	Kin-U	3605564	Pte Armsby	

21 January	Kabwet	5343619	Cpl Fruen	
26 January	Kabwet	6021413	Pte Leggett	
28 January	Kabwet	5348528	Sgt Spicer	
30 January	Kabwet	5334219	Sgt Barrett	
30 January	Kabwet	6019091	L/Cpl Burgess	
30 January	Kabwet	5339844	Cpl Bailey	
30 January	Kabwet	3604922	Pte Lea	
5 February	Yeshin	5336340	CQMS Freed	Accidentally
5 February	Yeshin	14305605	Pte Hillier	killed by air drop
26 February	Ywathit	14754336	Pte Webb	
26 February	Ywatgut	14407034	Pte Downes	
5 March	Udein	5347440	Pte Crook	
6 March	Madaya	5347906	Pte Allwright	
10 March	Mandalay	14340725	Pte Dodd MM	
10 March	Mandalay	5340913	L/Cpl Brown	
10 March	Mandalay	14577808	Pte Jenns	
11 March	Mandalay	5340873	L/Cpl Paget	
15 March	Mandalay	14295333	L/Cpl Boyle	
17 March	Mandalay	14722278	Pte Collicott	
21 March	South of Mandalay	3857861	Pte Ravenscroft	
10 April	Wundwin	4979237	Sgt Wynne	
5 May	Toungoo	14642900	Pte Adkins	
7 May	Toungoo	6028001	Pte Murray	

APPENDIX 2

7 Died of Wounds				
Date	Place	Number	Name	Remarks
4 January	Tantabin	5622057	Pte Briggs	
7 January	Kin-U	5439465	L/Cpl Heath	
30 January	Kabwet	14385503	Pte Birch	
17 February	Kyaukmyaung	5337800	L/Cpl Gill	Accidental
10 March	Mandalay	?	Pte Cullen	
13 March	Mandalay	5351848	Pte Fabray	
14 March	Mandalay	5346450	Sgt Heywood DCM	
1 Missing, Believed Killed				
Date	Place	Number	Name	Remarks
6 March	Madaya	5114812	L/Cpl Dale	

1944/45
Memories of Burma

"Ship me somewhere east of Suez, where the
            best is like the worst.
Where there aren't no ten commandments an' a man
            can raise a thirst;
For the temple bells are callin', an' it's there that
            I would be -
By the old Moulmein Pagoda looking lazy
            at the sea."

Rudyard Kipling "Mandalay"

The Royal Berkshire Regiment

19th Indian (Dagger) Division

14th Army

Index

(All page numbers in italics refer to illustrations)